MAGICAL SITES

MAGICAL SITES

WOMEN TRAVELERS
IN 19TH CENTURY LATIN AMERICA

EDITED BY
MARJORIE AGOSÍN & JULIE H. LEVISON

WHITE PINE PRESS • BUFFALO, NEW YORK

P.O. Box 236, Buffalo New York 14201

Acknowledgments: Tristán, Flora. "Travels Through Peru," from *Peregrinations of a Pariah.* London: Virago, 1986. Translated, edited and introduced by Jean Hawkes. Translation and introduction copyright ©1986 by Jean Hawkes. Reprinted with the kind permission of Jean Hawkes.

Rousier, Ana du. Selections from *The Life of Ana du Rousier,* used by kind permission of Paz Riesco, RSSJ. Translated by Mary G. Berg. Translation copyright ©1999 by Mary G. Berg. Printed with the kind permission of Mary G. Berg.

Gorriti, Juana Manuela. Selections from *El mundo de los recuerdos* and *Sueños y realidades.* Translated by Mary G. Berg. Translation copyright ©1999 by Mary G. Berg. Printed with the kind permission of Mary G. Berg.

Beltrán, María de la Merced. Selections from *La Havane.* Translated by Janice Molloy. Translation copyright ©1999 by Janice Molloy. Printed with the kind permission of Janice Molloy.

Publication of this book was made possible, in part, by grants from the National Endowment for the Arts, the New York State Council on the Arts, and Wellesley College.

Book design: Elaine LaMattina

Cover image: Detail from a painting by Remedios Varo.
Used by permission of the Art Museum of the Americas, Organization of American States.

Printed and bound in the United States of America

1   3   5   7   9   10   8   6   4   2

Library of Congress Cataloging-in-Publication Data
Magical sites : women travelers in 19th century Latin America / edited by Marjorie Agosín & Julie H. Levison.
    p.   cm.
Text in English with some selections translated from French, German, and Spanish.
Contents: Travels through Chile, 1822 / Mary Caldecott Graham — Travels through Argentina, Peru, and Bolivia, 1830 / Juana Manuela Gorriti — Travels through Peru, 1833 / Flora Tristan — Travels through Mexico, 1843 / Frances Erskine Inglis Calderón de la Barca — Travels through Cuba, 1844 / María de la Merced Beltrán — Travels through the West Indies, 1850 / Nancy Prince — Travels through Chile, 1853 / Ana du Rousier and Sacred Heart Nuns — Travels through the Brazils, 1855 / Ida Pfeiffer — Travels through Central America and Mexico, 1884 / Helen Sanborn — Travels through Nicaragua, 1887 / Dora Hort.
ISBN 1-877727-94-6 (alk. paper)
    1. Latin America—Description and travel. 2. Latin America—Social life and customs—19th century. 3. Women travelers—Latin America—History—19th century. 4. Visitors, Foreign—Latin America—History—19th century. 5. Travelers' writings. I. Agosín, Marjorie. II. Levison, Julie H.
F1409.M22 1999   99-11291
980—dc21   CIP

In memory of my grandmother, Josefina, who crossed the Andes on a mule, and my grandfather, Joeseph, who taught me that to travel is to dream.

–M.A.

In memory of my grandmother, Anna, who recounted to me memories of life in Europe, and to the memory and spirit of my great-grandmother, Haya, who taught me the meaning of women's travel when she crossed the Atlantic to bring her children to this new country.

–J.L.

Contents

INTRODUCTION

People with eternity, broth of a subtropical blood, bodies alive with the sea and the light of mountain peaks, dance their vigorous pride. They dance an ancient language beneath mountains that told them to be decorous and beside a sea that taught them to be wild.

—Gabriela Mistral
Elegies to the Land of Chile

From the fiery vapors that rise from the lakes of dormant Andean volcanoes to the green Patagonian mists that sweep up from the Antarctic tip, the land and water of Latin America tempt the uncommon woman to a foreign terrain. The magical sites of pre-Columbian civilizations still exist, and a large part of the mystical lure of the southern hemisphere is its rich indigenous culture. The cultures of the Incas of Peru, the Aztecs of Mexico and the Arauncanians of Chile fused with the *mestizo* culture of European and Latino ancestry create a spectrum of traditions, stories, and cultural icons that weave together a unique and memorable history. Only now are the cultures of Latin America being understood as part of a pluralistic and complex region that encompasses a history of travel, migration, and colonization.

Any traveler walking down the cobblestone streets of Minas Gerais, Brazil, or in the Chiloé Province of Southern Chile will be enchanted by the people. It is as if this part of the world follows a structure that is independent of the casting of dawn or the setting of the sun. The eccentricities of the continent whisper to you through the passion of dance, be it the *cueca* or the magnetic tango, and in the magical realism captured by a Gabriel García Márquez story. This land offers challenges, fantasy, and adventure for the daring traveler. Yet to be a female traveler in the Latin America continent means more than just traveling and exploring the world. Throughout the ages, journeys have been tied to gender, class, and historical events, and few women were given the opportunity to travel. Those who did were not only pioneers in travel but also revolutionaries and inspirational sources for other women who were unable to finish the defiant journey to liberation.

Traveling, for women, has been forever associated with a forbidden mystery. It was unheard of for a woman to travel alone, and women in the nineteenth century traveled out of a sense of duty or defiance. In Latin America, one often hears stories of intrepid women adventurers, the hazy deeds of entire families that traveled in search of a haven, as well as stories of seafaring women, who, alone, embarked in third-class vessels to meet with their relatives in new lands. Listening in on the conversations of elders, I recall my Chilean grandmother saying, "Yes, she traveled *alone!*" and a chorus of "decent" women would echo her comment with, "My God, she traveled *alone!* My God!"

Historically, travel has been a metaphor for women's true liberation. For women, travel presupposes fear, danger, and adventure, all emotions that were prohibited to women. It is customary to visualize the great travelers of history, from Marco Polo to Paul Thoreaux, as great men whose trips also had the social function of telling the world about the power and adventures of the patriarchy. The women, following the ancient code of chivalry, waited, like the faithful Penelope, to be told about the journeys. But there were women who had a spirit of adventure and who were determined to embark on their own odysseys.

Since women have traditionally been responsible for maintaining the social matrix at home when the men are at war or traveling, the simple fact of female travel becomes an act of resistance to feminine social responsibilities. It has only been in the modern era of the late twentieth century that women have been able to loosen the fetters of domesticity and pursue their individual interests and pleasures without having a social stigma cast upon them. Yet even today, the image of the woman who is accountable only for herself and her travel bag still evokes a shudder in some quarters.

Traveling embodies a journey for the imagination and the possibility of creating a world of experiences, allowing women to tell of their own adventures instead of being mere receptacles for their male counterparts' stories. Traveling also allows women to witness life first-hand, to become accountable for their own histories, their own destinies.

In the nineteenth century, a few brave women crossed Cape Horn in pursuit of and in accordance with their fate. Finally, the voices of women travelers can be heard through their writings, and the joys and sorrows that these women felt during their journeys are revealed. But we still know little about women travelers, for many times women were not provided with the education that would enable them to record their journeys for posterity or they were denied permission to express their experiences. We know little about the few women who accompanied Christopher Columbus because they were not allowed to interpret the reality that surrounded them. Thus, the women's point of view was never recorded in the early chronicles, and they remain invisible.

In a time when women could not travel freely unless escorted by a man or in a large group, an unaccompanied woman traveler had to rely on skill and the art of deception, just as Penelope did to avoid the barrage of supplications for marriage from her suitors. Thus, disguised as men, a few brave women boarded ships of the high seas and entered the business of piracy. Mary Read is one such example. Born out of wedlock, Mary ran away from home at a young age. Masked in male garb, she eventually joined a Dutch merchant ship until it was taken over by "Calico Jack," the nefarious pirate formally known as Captain Jack Rackham. She joined his crew until their ship was captured off the coast of Jamaica in October of 1720. The entire crew was put into jail and sentenced to death. English law at the time forbade the hanging of pregnant women, and upon discovering she was pregnant, Mary was given clemency. She remained in jail, however, and later died there of an illness.

Even a century after Mary Read, society remained steadfast in reminding women of their place in the world: the home. The corset, wire hoop dresses, and foot binding, all part of a woman's daily dress, reminded women to moderate their breath, to regress and traverse the straight path society had laid down for them. Other than the few women who possessed a dowry, most women had no money of their own. Women were objects of possession rather than possessors. They empowered an otherwise subservient role by developing and relying on a heightened sense of creativity and spirituality, and they found their pleasure in romantic novels, plays, and art—most of which were created by men.

Before the advent of railways, cars, and planes, women simply relied on their own stamina to walk or ride horseback as means of transportation. If a woman had sufficient resources, she could pay a servant to carry her in a hammock. With the invention of the steam engine in the early nineteenth century and the development of the internal-combustion engine in the beginning of the twentieth century, the means of transportation dramatically improved, giving women a chance to leave their native lands and travel on their own. A great era of women and their voyages began.

Travel in the nineteenth century provided women with the opportunity to envision a life beyond the idealized, contrived worlds about which they read. With this new outlet drawing women out from the locus of the home, women gained an active role in their existence and a sense of social agency. However, financial resources, education, and social status still made travel unavailable to most women.

For the aristocratic woman traveler, going on an intercontinental voyage was simply an excursion, a dynamic tangent to the monotony of life. While enroute to Chile from their native land of England, the husband of Mary Graham Caldecott died, leaving her alone in an unfamiliar land. Caldecott moved into a cottage given to her by her friends near the port of Valparaiso and began an exploration of her environment and its unique flora and fauna. On the red-soiled hills and in her *arboleda*, or orchard, Mrs. Caldecott found the prickly pear, *tunia*; the indigenous tree, *Quillai*, surrounded her flower garden. Her detailed description of the land shows Caldecott's tremendous reverence for Chile as a sanctuary that allowed her the pleasure of a beautiful landscape while exploring her own identity as widow and woman transformed.

Flora Tristán, an early feminist, left her native land for freedom and adventure. Tristán left Bordeaux, France, on April 7, 1833, for a stormy, one-hundred-and-thirty-three-day voyage on the steamship *Mexicain* to Peru. The only woman among the crew and four passengers, Ms. Tristán had to rely on her inner strength to sustain her through a delirious first twelve days of terrible seasickness. The crew tried to mitigate her discomfort, but she said the only thing that kept her going was "an inner voice that told me that I was not going to die."

One of the more revealing passages of Ms. Tristán's journal is her chapter on Arequipa, Chile, where she visits her cousin Doña Carmen. As they visit, they must sit through the rhythmic yet always startling *terremotos*, or earthquakes, that tremble through this volcanic region. Doña Carmen shrieks out her abhorrence for the country, but she says that she can never leave because a lack of money of her own leaves her dependent on the status quo. Ms. Tristán explains that she, too, is poor but fled France because "...freedom is really a matter of will. Those to whom God has given a will strong enough to overcome every obstacle are free, whereas those whose will is weak and yields to opposition are slaves and would still be slaves even if some freak of fortune placed them upon a throne." Even though domesticity constricts a woman's independent choices, Flora Tristán proves that determination delivers true, divine freedom.

María de la Merced Beltrán was born into the Cuban aristocracy but left her homeland at the age of twelve. Her account is unique in that she describes, in letters written to her daughter, the overwhelming emotions she felt upon returning to Cuba at the age of fifty-five.

International travel was not available only to those who could afford a life of leisure. Entering the religious order provided many women with a social outlet other than marriage. As "soldiers of Christ," women like Nancy Prince and the Reverend Mother Ana du Rousier left behind families and communities for a higher spiritual calling. Both women were driven by the goal of spreading the word of God to the native people so that they could transcend physical and emotional barriers. French nun Ana du Rousier's journal details her travel experiences across the Isthmus of Panama in 1853 and eventually to Chile, where she leads a caravan to establish schools. Traveling was very difficult because it was a challenge to change clothing in extremes of weather, to sleep, or even go to the bathroom in privacy while accompanied by foreign men. Tension with the native guides and a mutually-profound racial mistrust always made the nuns question whether they would even survive their travels.

Nancy Prince's vision is unique in that she is a black woman, who in 1850, after a request from Reverend Ingraham, left Boston to improve the spiritual, moral, and social condition of the West Indian natives, especially the children. As a part of the missionary team, Ms. Prince never considered herself academically talented, but she believed she was qualified to instill a reverence for God in those with whom she came in contact. The community so longed for her to stay that when she wanted to return to New England there was a violent insurrection and she put her life in jeopardy to return to Boston.

Some women became active participants in the travel experience while accompanying male family members on business. Frances Erskine Inglis Calderón de la Barca, Scottish by birth and American by upbringing, traveled with her husband, Angel

Calderón de la Barca, Spanish minister to the recently-liberated Mexico. In the passages we've selected, Fanny Calderón de la Barca writes of visiting numerous churches and cathedrals during Holy Week. Having a common language with the natives of Mexico made it possible for her to converse with them, and she describes Mexico with an affectionate eye. A common cultural background enables her to relate to Mexico's numerous ambiguities and very diverse spirit. Coffee heiress Helen Sanborn accompanied her father on a visit to coffee plantations in Guatemala. She was more than mere traveling companion, however: she learned Spanish so she could act as his translator.

Some women traveled for the pure exhilaration of the risk and danger that comes with exploring new territory. Ida Pfeiffer climbed the grand Cordillera of the Andes mountains in 1855. Despite the thinning air, unpredictable extremes of weather, lack of shelter, and sheer fear of death, Pfeiffer traversed the stony path to reach the summit at nearly 16,000 feet. At the pinnacle of this mountain she placed a stone, in memory of an Englishman who was murdered in the journey to the apex of Chimborazo, on a pile of stones left by travelers who had reached this point before her. In doing so, Ida Pfeiffer left an indelible reminder of her presence as one of the first women to climb the Andes Mountains.

Some women, such as Juana Gorriti, became itinerants as they crisscrossed the South American continent in search of political freedom and respect. Her accounts show how she strives to adapt to the new land rather than to judge it. She wanted to understand the country she was in, and although her home in her native Argentina was more similar to homes in the great cities of England and France, her texts are centered around the natural world. She integrates her soul with the nature that surrounds her: "Each tree, each leaf, each turn in the path awoke a whole host of painful memories in my soul. From the branches of the carob tree, which now showers my head with flowers."

Creativity and flexibility were essential qualities that enabled Dora (Mrs. Alfred) Hort, to travel by mule through the Nicaraguan countryside in 1887. The only saddle available to Ms. Hort was designed for males, which forced her to either straddle the mule or sit uncomfortably with both legs to one side. As a pioneer traveler, Ms. Hort was constantly reminded of harsh reality: travel and free movement were not part of a woman's sphere of existence.

Each of these travel accounts shows how women from diverse parts of the world thought about travel and the nations they left behind, and how they became acclimated to their new surroundings. The voices here belong to adventurers who crossed the borders of tradition to see, describe, understand, and interpret the world around them.

Travel, for women, continues to be shrouded in danger and mystery. This anthology began as a search for early women travelers to the Latin American continent. We wanted to know who they were and what they were searching for, and we attempted to gather highly significant, yet virtually unknown, female travelers, so the reader could understand what traveling meant to women. One of the main goals of this anthology is to give the sort of women's writing that has traditionally been trivialized, i.e., diaries, travel journals, and letters, the literary and social value it so rightly deserves. Some of these words have never before seen the light of day: we found Ana du Rosier's journals in a musty convent library in Chile. Our objective has been to make this anthology as eclectic and vibrant as the women themselves. The possibility of finding in one volume the visions, images, and accounts of travel by women of diverse culture and nationality allows us to explore the way in which the European eye had defined "otherness," and in many of the pieces we see how the ideological spirit of colonialism influenced the writers' vision of the Americas. We see, too, how contact with this new world influenced the women.

This anthology unites the multifaceted voices and visions of European, North American, and Latin American women. *Women Travelers in 19th Century Latin America* is a meditation on what it means not only to travel but to write about this experience, to become a chronicler of one's own time and place and to record what one saw through a woman's eyes—which implies being empowered, autonomous, and ultimately free.

—Marjorie Agosín

MAGICAL SITES

RESIDENCE IN CHILE

Mary Graham Caldecott

Mary Graham Caldecott (1788-1843), also known as Maria Dundas Graham and Lady Maria Colcott, is considered to be one of Chile's most distinguished and original 19th century writers. A British aristocrat, she married British sea captain Sir Thomas Graham, who died on board the ship that was carrying them to Chile in 1822. Upon her arrival in Valparaiso, the young widow decided to settle there and became a keen observer of the Chilean lifestyle, the natural environment, and the flora and fauna of the Pacific region. Her insights into Chilean culture reveal that Graham was an avid observer of social norms and customs. Like her contemporary, Fanny Calderón de la Barca, her gaze is not that of an intruder but of a participant in Chile's development and history.

Her text, *Journal of a Residence in Chile,* is virtually unknown in the English-speaking world. Other writings by Mary Graham Caldecott include *Journals of a Residence in India* (1812); *Letters on India* (1814); *Three Months in the Mountains East of Rome* (1819); *Memoirs of the Life of Poussin* (1820); *Journal of a Voyage to Brazil and Residence there During Part of the Years of 1821, 1822, 1823* (1824); *Journal of a Residence in Chile During the Year 1822, and a Voyage from Chile to Brazil in 1823* (1824); *History of Spain* (1828); *Little Arthur's History of England* (1835); *Essays toward the History of Painting* (1836); *A Scripture Herbal* (1842).

VALPARAISO

Monday, 29th.—This has been a day of trial. Early in the morning the new captain's servants came on board to prepare the cabin for their master's reception. I believe, what must be done is better done at once. Soon after breakfast, Captain Ridgely, of the United States' ship, *Constellation*, brought Mrs. and Miss Hogan, the wife and daughter of the American consul, to call and to offer all the assistance in their power; and told me, that the Commodore had delayed the sailing of his frigate, the *Constellation*, in order that she might carry letters from the *Doris* round Cape Horn, and would delay it still farther if I wished to avail myself of the opportunity to return home immediately. I was grateful, but declined the offer. I feel that I have neither health nor spirits for such a voyage just yet.

Immediately afterwards, Don Jose Ignacio Zenteno, the governor of Valparaiso, with two other officers, came on board on a visit of humanity as well as respect. He told me that he had appointed a spot within the fortress where I may "bury my dead out of my sight," with such ceremonies and honours as our church and service demand, and has promised the attendance of soldiers. All this is kind, and it is liberal.

At four o'clock I received notice that Mrs. Campbell, a Spanish lady, the wife of an English merchant, would receive me into her house until I could find a lodging, and I left the ship shortly afterwards.

I hardly know how I left it, or how I passed over the deck where one little year ago I had been welcomed with such different prospects and feelings.

I have now been two hours ashore. Mrs. Campbell kindly allows me the liberty of being alone, which is kinder than any other kindness she could show.

April 30th.—This afternoon I stood at my window, looking over the bay. The captain's barge, of the *Doris*, brought ashore the remains of my indulgent friend, companion, and husband. There were all his own people, all those of the *Blossom* and of the American ships, and their flags joined and mingled with those of England and of Chile; and their musicians played together the hymns fit for the burial of the pure in heart; and the procession was long, and joined by many who thought of those far off, and perhaps now no more and by many from respect to our country; and I believe, indeed I know, that all was done that the pious feelings of our nature towards the departed demand; and if such things could soothe such a grief as mine they were not wanting.

But my mind has bowed before him in whose hand are the issues of life and death. And I know that I cannot stay long behind, though my life were lengthened to the utmost bounds of human being. And I trust, that when I am called to another state of existence, I may be able to say, "Oh Death, where is thy sting? Oh Grave, where is thy victory?"

May 6th.—I have been very unwell. Meantime my friends have procured a small house for me at some distance from the port, and I am preparing to remove to it.

9th of May, 1822.—I took possession of my cottage at Valparaiso; and felt indescribable relief in being quiet and alone. By going backwards and forwards twice between Mrs. Campbell's and my own house, I have seen all that is to be seen of the exterior of the town of Valparaiso. It is a long straggling place, built at the foot of steep rocks which overhang the sea, and advance so close to it in some places as barely to leave room for a narrow street, and open in others so as to admit of two middling squares, one of which is the market-place, and has on one side the governor's house, which is backed by a little fort crowning a low hill. The other square is dignified by the *Iglesia Matriz*, which, as there is no bishop here, stands in place of a cathedral. From these squares several ravines or *quebradas* branch off; these are filled with houses, and contain, I should imagine, the bulk of the population, which I am told amounts to 15,000 souls; further on there is the arsenal, where there are a few slips for building boats, and conveniences for repairing vessels; but all appearing poor; and still farther is the outer fort, which terminates the port on that side. To the east of the governor's house, the town extends half a quarter of a mile or a little more, and then joins its suburb, the Almendral, situated on a flat, sandy, but fertile plain, which the receding hills leave between them and the sea. The Almendral extends to three miles in length, but is very narrow; the houses, like most of those in the town, are of one story. They are all built of unburned bricks, whitewashed and covered with red tiles; there are two churches, one of the Merced, (The royal, religious, and military order of the Merced was instituted by the king Don

Jayme el Conquistador for the purpose of redeeming captives.) rather handsome, and two convents, besides the hospital, which is a religious foundation. The Almendral is full of olive groves, and of almond gardens, whence it has its name; but, though far the pleasantest part of the town, it is not believed to be safe to live in it, lest one should be robbed or murdered, so that my taking a cottage at the very end of it is rather wondered at than approved. But I feel very safe, because I believe no one robs or kills without temptation or provocation; and as I have nothing to tempt thieves, so I am determined not to provoke murderers.

My house is one of the better kind of really Chilean cottages. It consists of a little entrance-hall, and a large sitting room six-teen feet square, at one end of which a door opens into a little dark bedroom, and a door in the hall opens into another a lit-tle less. This is the body of the house, in front of which, look-ing to the south-west, there is a broad veranda. Adjoining, there is a servants' room, and at a little distance the kitchen. My land-lord, who deals in horses, has stables for them and his oxen, and several small cottages for his peons and their families, besides storehouses all around. There is a garden in front of the house, which slopes down towards the little river that divides me from the Almendral, stored with apples, pears, almonds, peaches, grapes, oranges, olives, and quinces, besides pump-kins, melons, cabbages, potatoes, French beans, and maize, and a few flowers; and behind the house the barest reddest hill in the neighbourhood rises pretty abruptly. It affords earth for numerous beautiful shrubs, and is worn in places by the con-stant tread of the mules, who bring firewood, charcoal, and veg-etables to the Valparaiso market. The interior of the house is clean, the walls are whitewashed, and the roof is planked, for stucco ceilings would not stand the frequent earthquakes, of which we had one pretty smart shock tonight. No Valparaiso native house of the middling class boasts more than one window, and that is not glazed, but generally secured by carved wooden or iron lattice-work; this is, of course, in the public sitting-room; so that the bedrooms are perfectly dark: I am considered fortunate in having doors to mine, but there is none between the hall and the sitting-room, so I have made bold to hang up a curtain, to the wonder of my landlady, who cannot understand my finding no amusement in watching the motions of the servants or visitors who may be in the outer room.

May 10th.—Thanks to my friends both ashore and in the frigate, I am now pretty comfortably settled in my little home. Everybody has been kind; one neighbour lends me a horse, another such furniture as I require: nation and habits make no difference. I arrived here in need of kindness, and I have received it from all.

I have great comfort in strolling on the hill behind my house; it commands a lovely view of the port and neighbouring hills. It is totally uncultivated, and in the best season can afford but poor browsing for mules or horses. Now most of the shrubs are leafless, and it is totally without grass. But the milky tribe of trees and shrubs are still green enough to please the eye. A few of them, as the lobelia, retain here and there an orange or a crimson flower; and there are several sorts of parasitic plants, whose exquisitely beautiful blossoms adorn the naked branches of the deciduous shrubs, and whose bright green leaves, and vivid red and yellow blossoms shame the sober grey of the neighbouring olives, whose fruit is now ripening. The red soil of my hill is crossed here and there by great ridges of white half marble, half sparry stone; and all its sides bear deep marks of winter torrents; in the beds of these I have found pieces of green stone of a soft soapy appearance, and lumps of quartz and coarse granite. One of these water-courses was once worked for gold, but the quantity found was so inconsiderable, that the proprietor was glad to quit the precarious adventure, and to cultivate the *chacra*, or gardenground, which joins to mine, and whose produce has been much more beneficial to his family.

I went to walk in that garden, and found there, besides the fruits common to my own, figs, lemons, and pomegranates, and the hedges full of white cluster roses. The mistress of the house is a near relation of my landlady, and takes in washing, but that by no means implies that either her rank or her pretensions are as low as those of a European washerwoman. Her mother was possessed of no less than eight *chacras*; but as she is ninety years old, that must have been a hundred years ago, when Valparaiso was by no means so large a place, and consequently *chacras* were less valuable. However, she was a great proprietor of land; but, as is usual here, most of it went to portion off a large family of daughters, and some I am afraid to pay the expenses of the gold found on the estate.

The old lady, seeing me in the garden, courteously invited me to walk in. The veranda in front of the house is like my own, paved with bricks nine inches square, and supported by rude wooden pillars, which the Chileno architects fancy they have carved handsomely; I found under it two of the most beautiful boys I ever saw, and a very pretty young woman, the grandchildren of the old lady. They all got up from the bench eager to receive me, and show me kindness. One of the boys ran to fetch his mother, the other went to gather a bunch of roses for me, and the daughter Joanita, taking me into the house gave me some beautiful carnations. From the garden we entered immediately into the common sitting room, where, according to custom, one low latticed window afforded but a scanty light. By the window, a long bench covered with a sort of coarse Turkey carpet made here, runs nearly the length of the room, and before this a wooden platform, called the *estrada*, raised about six inches from the ground, and about five feet broad, is covered with the same sort of carpet, the rest of the floor being bare brick. A row of high-backed chairs occupies the opposite side of the room. On a table in a corner, under a glass case, I saw a little religious baby work,—a waxen Jesus an inch long, sprawls on a waxen Virgin's knee, surrounded by Joseph, the oxen and asses, all of the same goodly material, decorated with moss and sea shells. Near this I observed a pot of beautiful flowers, and two pretty-shaped silver utensils, which I at first took for implements of worship, and then for inkstands, but I discovered that one was a little censer for burning *pastile*, with which the young women perfume their handkerchiefs and *mantos*, and the other the vase for holding the infusion of the herb *Paraguay*, commonly called *matte*, so universally drank or rather sucked here. The herb appears like dried senna; a small quantity of it is put into the little case with a proportion of sugar, and sometimes a bit of lemon peel, the water is poured boiling on it, and it is instantly sucked up through a tube about six inches long. This is the great luxury of the Chilenos, both male and female. The first thing in the morning is a *matte*, and the first thing after the afternoon *siesta* is a *matte*. I have not yet tasted of it, and do not much relish the idea of using the same tube with a dozen other people.

I was much struck with the appearance of my venerable neighbour; although bent with age she has no other sign of infirmity; her walk is quick and light, and her grey eyes sparkle with intelligence. She wears her silver hair, according to the custom of the country, uncovered, and hanging down behind in one large braid; her linen shift is gathered up pretty high on her bosom, and its sleeves are visible near the wrist: she has a petticoat of white woolen stuff, and her gown of coloured woolen is like a close jacket, with a full-plaited petticoat attached to it, and fastened with double buttons in front. A rosary hangs round her neck, and she always wears the *manto* or shawl, which others only put on when they go out of doors, or in cold weather. The dress of the granddaughter is not very different from that of a French woman, excepting that the *manto* supersedes all hats, caps, capotes, and turbans. The young people, whether they fasten up their tresses with combs, or let them hang down, are fond of decorating them with natural flowers, and it is not uncommon to see a rose or a jonquil stuck behind the ear or through the earring.

Having sat some time in the house, I accepted Joanita's proposal to walk in the garden; part of it was already planted with potatoes, and part was ploughing for barley, to be cut as green meat for the cattle. The plough is a very rude implement, such as the Spanish brought it hither three hundred years ago; a piece of knee timber, shod at one end with a flat plate of iron, is the plough, into which a long pole is fixed by means of wedges; the pole is made fast to the yoke of the oxen, who drag it over the ground so as to do little more than scratch the surface. (I recollect a bit of antique mosiac, I think, but am not sure, in the Villa Albani, near Rome, representing just such a plough, and so yoked; the oxen are represented kicking, as if stung by a gadfly.) As to a harrow, I have not seen or heard of one. The usual substitute for it being a bundle of fresh branches, which is dragged by a horse or ox, and if not heavy enough, stones, or the weight of a man or two, is added. The pumpkins, lettuces, and cabbages, are attended with more care: ridges being formed for them either with the original wooden spades of the country, or long-handled iron shovels upon the same plan. The greatest labour, however, is bestowed on irrigating the gardens, which is rendered indispensable by the eight months of dry weather in the summer. A multitude of little canals cross every field, and the hours for letting the water into them are regulated with reference to the convenience of the neighbours, through whose grounds the common stream passes. One part of every *chacra* is an *arboleda*, or orchard, however small, and few are without their little flower plot, where most of the common garden flowers of England are cultivated. The lupine both perennial and annual is native here. The native bulbous roots surpass most of ours in beauty, yet the strangers are treated with unjust preference. Roses, sweetpeas, carnations, and jasmine are deservedly prized; mignonette and sweetbriar are scarce, and honeysuckle is not to be procured. The scabiouss is called the widow's flower, and the children gathered their hands full of it for me.

From the flower-garden we went to the washing-ground, where I found a charcoal fire lighted on the brink of a pretty rivulet. On the fire was a huge copper vessel full of boiling water, and swimming in it there was a leaf of the prickly pear *(Cactus ficus Indicus)*, here called *tunia*; this plant is said to possess the property of cleansing and softening the water. Close by there stood a large earthen vessel, which appeared to me to be full of soap-suds, but I found that no common soap was among it. The tree called *Quillai*, which is common in this part of Chile, furnishes a thick rough bark, which is so full of soapy matter that a small piece of it wrapped in wool, moistened, and then beaten between two stones makes a lather like the finest soap and possesses a superior cleansing quality. All woolen garments are washed with it, and coloured woolen or silk acquires a freshness of tint equal to new by the use of it. I begged a piece of the dry bark; the inside is speckled with very minute crystals, and the taste is harsh like that of soda. In my walk home from the washing-ground, I had occasion to see specimens both of the wagons and carriages of Chile. The wheels, axletree, carriage, all are fastened together without a single nail or piece of iron. The wheels have a double wooden felly, placed so as that the joints in the one are covered by the entire parts of the other, and these are fastened together by strong, wooden pins; the rest is all of strong wooden frame-work; bound with hide, which being put on green, contracts and hardens as it dries, and makes the most secure of all bands. The flooring of both cart and coach consists of hide; the cart is tilted with canes and straw neatly wattled; the coach is commonly of painted canvas, nailed over a slight frame with seats on the sides, and the entrance behind. The coach is commonly drawn by a mule, though oxen are often used for the purpose; and always for the carts, yoked as for the plough. Oxen will travel hence to Santiago, upwards of ninety miles, with a loaded wagon in three days. These animals are as fine here as I ever saw them in any part of the world; and the mules particularly good. It is needless to say anything of the horses, whose beauty, temper, and spirit, are unrivaled, notwithstanding their small size.

11th May.–This morning, tempted by the exceeding fineness of the weather, and the sweet feeling of the air, I set out to follow the little water-course that irrigates my garden, towards its source. After skirting the hill for about a furlong, always looking down on a fertile valley, and now and then gaining a peep at the bay and shipping between the fruit trees, I heard the sound of falling water, and on turning sharp round the corner of a rock, I found myself in a *quebrada*, or ravine, full of great blocks of granite, from which a bright plentiful stream had washed the red clay as it leaped down from ledge to ledge, and fell into a little bed of sand glistening with particles of mica that looked like fairy gold. Just at this spot, where myrtle bushes nearly choked the approach, a wooden trough detained part of the rivulet in its fall, and led it to the course cut in the fall for the benefit of the cultivated lands on the side; the rest of the stream runs to the Santiago road, where meeting several smaller rills, it waters the opposite side of the valley, and finds its way to the shore, where it oozes through a sand-bank to the sea, close to a little cove filled with fishermen's houses. On ascending the ravine a little farther, I found at the top of the waterfall, a bed of white marble lying along on the sober grey rock; and beyond it, half concealed by the shrubs, the water formed a thousand little falls—

Through bushy brake and wild flowers blossoming,
And freshness breathing from each silver spring,
Whose scattered streams from granite basins burst,
Leap into life, and sparkling woo your thirst.

But this valley, like all those in the immediate neighbourhood of Valparaiso, wants trees. The shrubs, however, are beautiful, and mixed here and there with the Chilean aloe *(Pourretia Coarctata)*, and the great torch thistle, which rises to an extraordinary height. Among the humble flowers remarked varieties of our common garden flowers, caraway, fennel, sage, thyme, mint, rue, wild carrot, and several sorts of sorrel. But it is not yet the season of flowers; here and there only, a solitary fuchsia or andromeda was to be found;—but I did not want flowers,—the very feel of the open air, the verdure, the sunshine, were enough; and I doubly enjoyed this my first rural walk after being so long at sea.

May 30th.—I dined to-day in the port, with my very kind friends, Mr. Hogan, the American consul, and his wife and daughters; and met Captain Guise, lately of the Chileno naval service, together with his followers Dr. —— and Mr. ——. Captain Guise was exceedingly polite to me, and appears to be a good-natured gentleman like man. I have no doubt that, in the service, the technical and professional knowledge of Dr.—— and Mr.—— has been of infinite service, and that they have claims on the gratitude, to a certain degree, of all who love the cause of independence; but they neither possess the elevated tone of mind necessary for leading men and influencing council, nor information for guidance by precedent. In short, I must look upon them as adventurers, whose only aim has been to accumulate wealth in these rich provinces, without either the philanthropic or the chivalrous views which I am persuaded have accompanied the hopes of personal advantage in the minds of many of their fellow-labourers, in the great struggle for independence. To all whose views have been so bounded disappointment must be the consequence. Mere gold and silver scarcely render individuals rich; and nations they have in many cases rendered poor. Hence, Chile and Peru, who only possess money, and not money's worth, are far too poor to give adequate rewards to their foreign servants; and all that could rationally be anticipated was the precarious chance of Spanish prize-money. I feel convinced that the divisions that I hear have taken place in the squadron have arisen from the disappointment of such hopes too highly raised unless indeed, what I should shudder to think true, any English officers expected that their service in Chile would be only a kind of licensed buccaneering, where each should be a master of his own ship and his own actions, without rile or subordination. But the government wisely foresaw that danger; and the English naval code was adopted, and rigid subordination established the supreme command confided to able, firm, and honourable hands; and I fondly trust that the benefit of this sage measure will be permanently felt.

By letters from Lima received this day, it appears that Lord Cochrane had not gone on shore in Peru; that he lies in Callao bay, with his guns shotted; and that we may soon expect him here.

I had an opportunity to-day of observing how carelessly even sensible men make their observations in foreign countries, and on daily matters concerning them. A physician, at dinner, mentioned the medicinal qualities of the *culen (Cytisus Arboreus)*, and that it would be worth while to bring it into Chile, or at least to the neighbourhood of Valparaiso, to cultivate for the purpose of exportation. I was almost afraid to say, as I am a new-comer, that the country people had shown me a plant they called *culen*; but, on venturing to tell the gentleman so, he said it could not be because he never heard of it here. I went home, walked to the Quebrada, found the rocks on both sides covered with the best *culen*, and the inferior sort which grows much higher, not uncommon. Yet he is a clever man, and has resided some years in the country. This same *culen* is very agreeable as tea, and is said to possess antiscorbutic and antifebrile qualities, the smell of the dried leaves is pleasant, and a sweetish gum exudes from the flower-stalks. This gum is used by shoemakers instead of wax; and the fresh leaves formed into a salve with hogs' lard, are applied with good effect to recent wounds.

The mistakes about the *culen* put me in mind of Mrs. Barbauld's admirable tale, in the *Evenings at Home*, of "Eyes and no Eyes." How much we are obliged to that excellent woman, who with genius and taste to adorn the first walks of literature, gave up the greatest fame to do the greatest good, by forming the minds of the young, and leading them to proper objects of pursuit. I am proud to belong to the sex and nation, which will furnish names to engage the reverence and affection of our fellow-creatures as long as virtue and literature continue to be cultivated. As long as there are parents to teach and children to be taught, no father, no mother will hear with indifference the names of Barbauld, Trimmer, or Edgeworth. Even here, in this distant clime, they will be revered. The first stone is laid; schools are established, and their works are preparing to form and enlighten the children of another language and another hemisphere.

* * *

Monday, 9th.—One very slight shock; the day dull and cloudy; the thermometer at 65° Fahrenheit. In the evening I had a pleasant walk to the beach with Lord Cochrane; we went chiefly for the purpose of tracing the effects of the earthquake along the rocks at Valparaiso, the beach is raised about three feet, and some rocks are exposed, which allows the fisherman to collect the clam, or scallop shell-fish, which were not supposed to exist there before. We traced considerable cracks in the earth all the way between the house and the beach, about a mile, and the rocks have many evidently recent rents in the same direction: it seemed as if we were admitted to the secrets of nature's laboratory. Across the natural beds of granite, there are veins from an inch to a line in thickness. Most of these are quite filled up with white shiny particles, I suppose quartz, and in some places they even project a little from the face of the rock; others only begin to leave their sides coated, and have their edges rounded, but are not nearly filled. The cracks of this earthquake are sharp and new, and easily to be distinguished from older ones: they run, besides, directly under the neighboring hills, where the correspondent openings are much wider; and in some instances the earth has actually parted and fallen, leaving the stony base of the hills bare. On the beach, although it was high tide, many rocks, with beds of mussels, remain dry, and the fish are dead; which proves that the beach is raised about four feet at the Herradura. Above these recent shells, beds of older ones may be traced at various heights along the shore; and such are found near the summits of some of the loftiest hills in Chile, nay, I have heard, among the Andes themselves. Were these also forced upwards from the sea, and by the same causes? On our return, I picked up on the beach, in a little cove where there is a colony of fishermen, a quality of sand, or rather of iron dust, which is very sensible to the magnet. It exactly resembles some that was brought to me from the Pearl Islands lately. Here the rocks are of grey granite, and the soil is sand mixed with vegetable mould, and layers of pebbles and seashells; some of these upwards of fifty feet above the present beach. Nothing can be more lovely than the evening and morning scenery here. This evening, as we returned to the house, the snowy Andes were decked in hues of rose and vermilion; and the nearer hills in dazzling purple, streaming to the ocean, where the sun was setting in unclouded radiance.

Tuesday, 10th.—While sitting at dinner with Lord Cochrane, Messrs. Jackson, Bennet, and Orelle, we were startled by the longest and severest shock since the first great earthquake on

November 19th. Some ran out of the house (for we now inhabit a part of it), and I flew to poor Glennie's bed-side: it had brought on severe hemorrhage, which I stopped with laudanum. Soon afterwards we had a slighter shock, and again at half past three a prolonged one. The wind was most violent, the thermometer at 65°.

11th.—A loud explosion and severe shock at half past seven a.m.; another at ten; and then two, very slight.

12th.—A violent shock at noon, a slight one afterwards. As we were riding home to-day from a little tour by Valle Alegri and the Carices, we found a long strip or bed of sea-weed, and another of mussles, dead and very offensive; they had never been within reach of the tide since 19th November. It was as fine a day as I ever remember.

"On the surface of the deep, The winds lay only not asleep;" and as they stole through the woods of odoriferous shrubs, conveyed an almost intoxicating feeling to the sense. I cannot conceive a finer climate than that of Chile, or one more delightful to inhabit; and now I am accustomed to the trembling of the earth, even that seems a less evil than I could have imagined. Old Purchas' quaint description of Chile is as true as it appears singular from its antiquated garb.—"The poor valley," says he, speaking of Chile, "is so hampered between the tyrannical meteors and elements, as that shee often quaketh with feare, and in these chill fevers shaketh off and loseth her best ornaments. Arequipa, one of her fairest townes, by such disaster in the yeere 1582, fell to the ground. And sometimes the neighbour hilles are infected with this pestilent fever, and tumble down as dead in the plain; thereby so amazing the fearful rivers, that the runne out of their channels to seeke new, or else stand still with wonder, and the motive heare failing, fall into an uncouth tympany, their bellies swelling into spacious and standing lakes: the tides, seeing this, hold back their course, and dare not approach their sometime beloved streames by divers miles' distance, so that betwixt these two stools the ships come to ground indeed. The sicke earth thus having her mouth stopped, and her stomache overlaied, forceth new mouthes, whence she vomiteth streams of oppressing waters. I speake not of the beastes and men, which, in these civil warres of nature, must needes bee subject to devouring miserie."

*   *   *

January 3d.—To-day I set up the lithographic press in Lord Cochrane's tent to print the following address to the Chilenos, which we hope to get ready to-morrow.

> *"Lord Cochrane to the Inhabitants of Chile"*
> Chilenos—My Countrymen!
>
> The common enemy of America has fallen in Chile. Your tri-coloured flag waves on the Pacific, secured by your sacrifices. Some internal commotions agitate Chile: it is not my business to investigate their causes, to accelerate or retard their effects; but I can only wish the result that may be most favourable for all parties. Chilenos! You have expelled from your country the enemies of your independence: do not sully the glorious act by encouraging discord, and promoting anarchy, that greatest of evils. Consult the dignity to which your heroism has raised you; and if you must take any step to secure your national liberty, judge yourselves, act with prudence, and be guided by reason and justice.

It is now four years since the sacred cause of your independence called me to Chile: I assisted you to gain it; I have seen it accomplished; it only remains to preserve it.

I leave you for a time, in order not to involve myself in matters foreign to my duties, and for reasons concerning which I now remain silent, that I may not encourage party spirit.

Chilenos! You know that independence is purchased at the point of the bayonet. Know also, that liberty is founded on good faith, and on the laws of honour; and that those who infringe upon them are your only enemies,—among whom you will never find.

—Cochrane

Quintero. January 4th, 1823

Mr. C——, who understands the management of the press better than any of our party, has kindly volunteered to come and assist in taking the impressions from the stone.

I like this wild life we are living, half in the open air; every thing is an incident and as we never know who is to come, or what is to happen next, we have the constant stimulus of curiosity to bear us to the end of every day. The evening walk is the only thing we are sure of. Sometimes we trace the effects of the recent earthquake, and fancy they lead to marks of others infinitely more violent, and at periods long anterior to our knowledge. Often we have little other object than the mere pleasure of the earth, and air, and sky. Sometimes we go to the garden, where every thing is thriving beyond all hope. And we are busy collecting seeds of the wild plants of the country, though it is too early in the season to find many ripe.

TRAVELS IN BOLIVIA, ARGENTINA, AND PERU

Juana Manuela Gorriti

Born in the province of Salta, Argentina, Juana Manuela Gorriti (1818-1892) spent most of her long life traveling and writing. Her family left Argentina in 1831 for exile in Bolivia. At age fourteen, Juana Manuela Gorriti married a Bolivian army officer, Manuel Isidoro Belzú, who later became dictator of Bolivia. When she left him and established herself in Lima in the 1840s, she began to publish her stories and memoirs, and she soon became one of the best known and most esteemed writers of her time. Most of her writings appeared first in periodicals, but then circulated more widely in such collections (all published in Buenos Aires) as *Sueños y realidades* [Dreams and realities] of 1865, *Panoramas de la vida: colección de novelas, fantasías, leyendas y descripciones americanas* [Panoramas of life: collection of novels, fantasies, legends and American descriptions] of 1876, *Misceláneas: colección de leyendas, juicios, pensamientos, discursos, impresiones de viaje y descripciones americanas* [Miscellanies: collection of legends, opinions, thoughts, speeches, travel impressions and American descriptions] of 1878, *El mundo de los recuerdos* [The world of memories] of 1886 and *Lo íntimo* [The intimate story] of 1892, published just after her death. In addition to these collections, Gorriti's many other books of fiction, biography, recipes and memoirs also circulated widely. Ever restless and unsettled, Gorriti moved back and forth between Buenos Aires, Lima, and La Paz, and wrote many descriptions of her travel experiences as well as using them in her fiction.

A YOUNG MILITARY WIFE ADAPTS TO BOLIVIA.

In the 1830s, Gorriti moved from one town to another in Bolivia, following the movement of troops commanded by her husband. Her travel anecdotes provide glimpses of life in various Bolivian outposts and of Gorriti's early attempts to adapt to the customs she encounters in her travels. This selection is from "El banquete de la muerte" [Death's Banquet] in *El mundo de los recuerdos* [The world of memories] 289-293.

For three years now, I had been leading the nomadic life of a young military wife, and because the troops had moved frequently, I had lived in all the cities of the Republic: first in Tarija, the city of beautiful women; then in Sucre, the Athens of Bolivia; in Potosí, famous for its silver; in the legendary La Paz, hidden among mountain peaks and fertile valleys at the foot of Illimani; and now in Oruro, formerly rich and well populated, located between a Sanctuary and a Fortress.

I found myself living there when the campaign against Peru began, in which Bolivian troops supported the legitimate Peruvian government against Salaverry's revolution. I decided to stay there until the army returned.

Despite the rigors of the climate on that very high Andean plain, hard hit by snowstorms and thunderstorms, life in Oruro is extremely pleasant. Its society is a mixture of culture and idyllic simplicity, and strangers are welcomed into it with the most cordial warmth and generosity. I very quickly found myself surrounded by affectionate friends, and my salon was frequented by society's most select young people.

In honor of them, I organized a literary society which I named "The Gentlemen of the Golden Spurs" which gathered weekly for programs of readings, music and speech giving. All this, spiced with occasional forays into criticism, rich in spiritualism and in explorations of new horizons. These assemblies which took place in my home were pleasing to my sedentary tastes.

Exhausted by the tumultuous existence of La Paz and Chuquisaca, with all of their balls, banquets, dinners, and picnic excursions, I hoped that life in this little backwater town, far from the two noisy metropolitan centers, would be restful.

What wishful thinking! In this "little backwater town," in sitting rooms protected from the cold by heavy draperies, thick carpets and braziers of hot coals, a constant succession of lunches, teas, dinners and dances took place; here today, there tomorrow, everyone feasted and danced without a pause.

I had to say to myself: "When in Rome, do what the Romans do."

This was all very well; I could get used to people banqueting continually and dancing all the time, but they also drank a lot; and this was the most difficult custom for me to adapt to, a real pitfall in my determination to keep up with everything Oruran society offered.

My friends helped me to find a way around this difficulty. Swearing me to profound secrecy, they showed me a certain trick which allowed me, from then on, to keep right up with even the most determined drinkers. This magic trick was...a sponge.

Cleverly concealed in my handkerchief, I could put it up to my lips and it would absorb the contents of the many glasses of refreshments which were pressed upon us. We could thus remain fresh and serene, astonishing our companions, who never dreamed, poor men, that we could be deceiving them in this way. But even after perfecting this life-saving strategy, there was one situation which still represented a great danger. *Execution!*

"Execution" was as terrible a ceremony as its name suggests. The last guest to arrive at a party, banquet or other gathering, would be pounced upon and seated with great ceremony on a chair previously placed in the very center of the room.

There, with hands tied, the last-comer would be forced to drink: if he were a man, with each one of the ladies present: if a woman, with a chosen execution squadron, which meant a minimum of four inescapable glasses, held up to her lips by the four chosen executioners.

It was totally impossible to refuse or evade this punishment; no excuse would do. People were so eager to avoid being last, that there was rarely an Execution victim to be found: all the guests would rush to arrive on time, and would arrive together just before the designated time. When the hour sounded, everyone would crush in the door together, clinging to each other.

If anyone were missing, a committee went in search of the straggler. And woe to the one who was absent, if he were not sick in bed or out of town.

That was a tyrannical practice, but it rose out of hearty country comradeship, patriarchal simplicity, and the most cordial friendliness.

HOMESICK FOR ARGENTINA

Homesick and struggling with marital difficulties, Gorriti slipped across the border and made a clandestine visit to Salta in 1842. She then returned to her husband and two daughters in Bolivia. This selection is titled "Una ojeada a la patria" [A Glimpse of My Homeland], a section dated 1850, which prefaces the novel "Gubi Amaya," published in *La Revista de Lima* in 1862 and included in *Sueños y realidades* [Dreams and Realities] of 1865, Vol. I, 129-135.

It was a burning hot afternoon in October. The sky was darkened in the East by dense storm clouds, shot through by frequent bolts of lightning, but in the West, the fires of the setting sun were blazing. The electricity stirred up the leaves of the trees, which shuddered, producing a dull roar, like the distant sound of the sea. The air was suffocatingly hot. The monotone chirp of cicadas hidden in the shadows of vegetation could be heard, and flocks of birds of all colors and sizes brushed the tops of the trees with their rapidly moving wings as they fled before the storm, which was approaching with lugubrious majesty.

How can I express what was happening in my soul, while alone and on foot I crossed the forest along the very paths I had walked along in a previous era, in the company of my beloved and distinguished family which had since been torn from the nation of their birth by the hurricane of an unspeakable misfortune, decimated at the peak of their flowering by death, reduced now to five weak offspring who were scattered far apart from each other!

All the ideas that can torment the mind and destroy the heart flowed through my consciousness. I was walking along with my head bent down over my chest, absorbed in the most painful thoughts, when I raised my eyes and saw the trees thin out and realized that I was coming to the edge of the forest, and to the amphitheater-shaped meadow which surrounded the hill on the top of which our old home had stood.

I stopped suddenly. My heart throbbed wildly in my chest, and I was afraid of my solitude at that supreme moment, as though the gates of eternity were about to open before me.

Afterward, under the influence of a fascination similar to that which makes us open our eyes again after we have closed them in order to not look at a horrible sight, I crossed through the last stands of trees at a run.

My eyes gazed in indescribable delight and indescribable pain, at that enchanted panorama which, constantly present in my memory, unfolded itself before me at this moment.

This had been my entire universe in earlier times, and now only I had changed; everything else was just like it had been the day—the very instant—I had left it. The hills running along the meadow on the northern side were still green, heavily wooded, and covered with flowers which I used to skip about gathering, in that earlier time when I was happy and confident of the future. Towards the South, the river followed its course, gurgling over the same bed of sand and bright-colored stones. In front of me, on the solitary rock, stood the ruins of the Jesuits' castle, with its venerable tower, still intact and blackened by the last rays of the sun, outlined against the stormy sky. And then my eyes beheld the final sight, farther down, on the gentle slope of a hill: the lovely house my father had built, where I lived as a child. It gleamed as white and resplendent as in earlier times, when on returning from bathing, I would pause to gaze at it with the distracted attention of the happy person.

Each tree, each leaf, each turn in the path awoke a whole host of painful memories in my soul. From the branches of this carob tree, which now showers my head with flowers, I had pulled down a nest of baby birds and, after crying all night long, thinking of their mother's grief, I had gotten up at dawn to put them back.

That level plain that stretches out of sight leads to Ortega. We went there often, and we raced our horses over that green field, making them wheel around and rear up beside our mother's carriage, from which we could hear her crying out in fear at each new madness, uselessly exhorting us to be sensible, and inviting my sisters and me to come join her in the unbearable monotony of her coach. My poor mother! She had no presentiment then of the true dangers that already menaced her children in the future; she still did not perceive the black cloud of griefs and tears suspended above those smiling faces. How merciful You are, My God, when You hide the future from us! Thus she enjoyed long happy days among the flowers that hid the abyss that has devoured us.

Meanwhile the storm had manifested itself violently, draping its mourning veil over the hills and the plain.

But neither the raindrops splashing against my face nor the powerful voice of the hurricane, not even the terrible thunderclaps, nothing was sufficient to pull my soul from its painful contemplation. Standing there, immobile, with my hand pressed against my throbbing heart, leaning with the other hand against the trunk of an old tree, I had transported myself in spirit back to a past era, scenes from which presented themselves one after another to my grieving mind, like reflections in a magic mirror. There was my father, surrounded by his many children, in that beautiful gallery where, grouped all around him, hiding in the folds of his cape, we gazed out, with curiosity mixed with fear, at the torrents of water and the columns of flames that shot up as lightning hit trees in the forest. I could hear the cries of joy with which we greeted the first breeze, the first ray of sunlight that chased off the clouds and made the droplets of water hanging from the green leaves gleam like diamonds in a crown. I watched us all racing and leaping to hurry to the garden and the meadows to see how many flowers had opened, and whether the baby birds needed our intervention to restore a water-damaged nest, and how many foxes had been killed by the lightning.

Ah! What had become of all those brilliant young inhabitants of that Eden? Tadeo! Pedro! Celestina! Severa! Julián! Antonina! Teresa! What has happened to all of you?

And to each of these names, a lugubrious echo sounded in the depths of my heart: "Ask your question of the grave."

Of all those companions so full of life, whose hearts beat with youth and hope on the threshold of an immense and promising future, I was the only one to return, with my heart heavy, to weep, like the prophet of lamentations, upon the ruins of the past; and I was an outsider now in the paternal home at which I gazed. I could make no claim on what had been my parents' home: I owned not a single stone on which to rest my head. Everything had been exchanged for the bitter bread of a foreign land.

A gruff voice and a vigorous hand placed on my shoulder returned me to myself. A man of about fifty, tall and strong, with a brown and ruddy countenance, gray hair, black eyes, and bushy eyebrows, was standing at my side.

"Sir," he said, deceived by my clothing. "Do you like getting wet or are you trying to insult me?

"Me, Sir?" I answered, startled by that gesture of rough familiarity, and feeling my woman's heart throb in fear under the pistol belts which I had heroically strapped around my chest.

"Yes," he replied. "Here you are taking refuge under a tree when you are just a few steps from my home, as though you were in the Arabian deserts."

These words and the man's accent informed me that he was a Spaniard. He was the present owner of the property.

That invitation, as simple as it was benevolent, typical of the frank and generous character of the Spanish, produced a painful reaction in me. "My home," he had said, pointing to the house that held my cradle as an infant. I seemed to see myself disinherited yet again, and I felt as though the very walls of this dwelling rejected me, saying "Stranger, go away, we do not know you."

When I entered the house, gentle hospitable voices chased away my sad thoughts. The women in the family came out to meet me, and greeted me, welcoming me with friendly simplicity. They occupied themselves in alleviating my exhaustion with such tender solicitude, with such frank cordiality, that for a moment I doubted whether the past were a dream after all, and whether this family were not mine.

Ah! Only the exile, the invalid, the orphan and the pilgrim can appreciate what is most noble, generous and tender in the souls of my beautiful compatriots. Anyone in power finds them proud and untamable because, like the locked cover of the Holy Book, they guard the treasures of their heart for the helpless.

Daughters of the River Plate, guardian angels of that Eden sown with tombs, given over for so long to appalling slaughter, there is nothing comparable to your evangelical charity and your sublime abnegation. You put aside your own misfortunes in order to console those who suffer. As grieving mothers and wives, you suppress the sobs of your own mourning in order to find gentle words of hope for a prisoner, and even when you are yourselves proscribed and homeless, you go out onto the battlefields to rescue the dying from the buzzard's claws, and you bandage his wounds with your own clothing. May God bless you, and bear you in mind in the hour of the redemption of our unfortunate nation.

THE NORTHWEST

Gorriti yearned all her life to return to Salta, her birthplace and site of her happy childhood. She wrote many accounts of her travels to Northwestern Argentina in 1878 and 1886. This selection is part of an extensive account, "Romería a la tierra natal" [Pilgrimage to My Birthplace] published in *El mundo de los recuerdos*, pp. 9-20, 27-29.

The Banks of the Paraná

One who wishes to contemplate nature in its most joyous splendor, should go up this river on a summer day, just when the sun's rays, filtering through the dense foliage, illuminate the depths of the exuberant vegetation growing along its banks.

The pyramidal poplar, the swooning willow, the ceiba with its purple flowers, and a thousand other varieties of Guaraní flora, interweave their dense foliage, showing off colors of such vividness and extraordinary variety of shades, that the richest palate would be incapable of reproducing them.

Leaning over the rail of the pretty little steamship that cut through the current as quickly as a seagull, my ears still deafened by the noisy tumult of Buenos Aires, I rejoiced in the contemplation of that succession of landscapes, each more beautiful and peaceful than the next, that appeared, came close, came almost within my hand's reach, assaulting me with the perfume of their flowers, then slipped past and disappeared only to be replaced by new configurations, in an infinite series.

And little islands rose up, defying the racing current: one here, formed by the roots of a gigantic tree, its foliage alive with the voices of a world of winged denizens; over there, another made up of a group of fig trees, their branches bent so low that their biblical fruits dip into the water.

Where the river bends, and the current eddies, I see thatched farmhouses on the wide riverbank, surrounded by all the paraphernalia of country life: stables, barns, chickens, goats, and hitched to a fence a saddled horse paws the ground and prances impatiently, waiting for his owner, who is seated in the animated group gathered around the hearth, playing the guitar, cajoling his beloved with the verses of a sad lovesong.

Reminiscences

Night began to fall.

The pungent odors of the forest soothed my senses, bringing to mind the gentle light of distant memories.

"Orcones! Miraflores! Gualiama!" I murmured, taking a deep breath of the breeze scented with balsam. And the radiant mirages of the distant past loomed up before me in white visions...

A scrap of melody chased away those welcome memories.

The passengers, including the members of a wedding party, had gathered in the salon, and the notes of the piano, played by an artist, accompanied the delicious soprano of the bride, who celebrated her happiness with a love song.

Afterward, arm in arm with her beloved, she sang that beautiful duet with him, that precious jewel that Verdi created with love and included in the treasury of melodies which is *Hernani:* "Ah, morir potesi adesso...."

Those familiar and much loved lines changed the course of my reverie which soared on wings of music all the way back to the night when I first heard that enchanting song.

It was the night of a party in Lima, the magical City of Kings....

El Rosario

Two hours later the little steamship anchored at the dock of this port.

El Rosario looks like a suburb of Buenos Aires: the same houses, the same enchanting villas and teeming streets.

I was not seeing it in the present: I was imagining it in the future when it would spread itself out along the riverbanks and become a powerful metropolis...

My pilgrimage to my birthplace began between here and Córd.

Buenos Aires and El Litoral are European towns which seem transplanted to American soil, keeping their physiognomy, their tastes and their customs: these age-old traditions have beautified our cities and civilized our countryside.

But ah, that bronzed town filled my eyes and soul with an almost religious affection, with its picturesque gauchos, wearing their traditional *chiripá*, galloping along like centaurs, upholding the proud majesty of the Pampa in their bearing and in their appearance, a forthright people who, led by a hero, rose up one day and brought liberty to two nations on the other side of the Andes.

Córdoba

Emotional yearning attracted me to this city.

My father called it his spirit's homeland. It was there that he acquired the vast erudition that made him the oracle of his time, and for the sake of his memory, I wanted to visit this sacred place.

Thus it was with respectful devotion that my feet were led to the red sands of its streets. I looked with daughterly affection at its old buildings, regretting that my fleeting visit did not allow me to enter that venerated University from which so many geniuses have emerged to illuminate the American world.

Nevertheless, in the brief hours I spent in the scientific metropolis, my devotion to a dear memory led me to the cemetery where the inspired Eugenia Echenique lies in eternal rest.

A cluster of bright butterflies fluttered around the monument where her remains lie. It was as though they were luminous representations of that powerful intellect. I knelt down and prayed fervently before that tomb where so many hopes had been buried, and I left a laurel wreath I had made for Eugenia, in Buenos Aires, when the beautiful writer was at the peak of her resplendent power....

The rest of the trip went by between exclamations of pleasure and cries of admiration.

"What a wonderful landscape!"

"What a picturesque group of trees!"

"A carpet of flowers!"

"A carob tree covered with golden berries!"
"A *mistolar* with its red fruit!"
"A lark!"
"A turtledove!"
"An ostrich!"
"The luminous *tucu-tucus*!"
And thus we went from ecstasy to another until we arrived at the beautiful city of Tucumán, which I had imagined for so long in the mists of poetic daydreams.

Tucumán

The beloved city of poets was hidden from my eyes by a veil of rain, periodically ripped by lightning.

However, every little while, a wave of perfume of orange and lemon blossoms reached me, revealing that the orchards lay nearby.

The birds nesting in the treetops filled the dawn with their cooing and their melodies.

The sun, although hidden in dense clouds, infused the air with an ever more intense heat.

What a sweet sense of well-being this balsam-laden atmosphere instills!

Lulled by its soft auras impregnated with warm breezes and exquisite perfumes, I felt my soul suspended in a state of ineffably sweet peace, and for those moments, I felt as though I had only dreamt the griefs and storms of my life.

One day, finally, as night fell, the north wind, ever a harbinger of good weather, began to blow, clearing away the clouds, brushing them away in shreds like strips of gauze in the blue spaces set with stars.

The following morning a splendid February sun gilded the

white cupolas and the red roofs of the picturesque buildings; and farther off, an ocean of vegetation extended far into the distance, under the lustrously transparent blue sky.

The earth spread itself out emanating delicious aromas, and a gentle fresh breeze blew through the greenery of the gardens with a delicious rustle. One could imagine it as the gossiping of fairies.

The bells rang out in joyful peals; children set off rockets.

Multitudes of vendors of fruits, pastries and flowers, their arms open and baskets balanced on their heads, went up and down the streets advertising their wares in accents as musical as their rhythmic paces.

Groups of pretty young women strolled about, greeting each other with kisses and smiles as they passed their friends.

Toward afternoon, two beautiful women, relatives on my father's side of the family, came by to collect me in a carriage and took me on a tour of the city.

Tucuman fulfills one's dreamlike first impression: it is enchanting in every sense of the word. It is a picturesque mixture of older buildings and new construction, the more recent edifices adorned with graceful cornices and towers, and the older ones hiding their time-worn, crumbling and cracking walls under the exuberant vegetation that clings to every surface.

Looking back to the past

I did not wish to leave Tucuman without a visit to an important and venerated monument: the hall where the first Congress of liberated citizens declared American Independence.

My father took part in that illustrious assembly; he represented Salta, an invincible bastion which withstood, on its own, attacks by enemy forces throughout years of continuous fighting.

Moved by a sentiment of profound respect, of religious awe, I entered that sacred place which the kindness of its guardians opened to my view.

It is a large, dark room in an old building, facing onto the back of a patio that looks like a field because of its size and because it is covered with grass.

Six oak beams hold up the roof, damaged by all the years of rains. Tall weeds grow by its doorsteps; its yellowish-white walls are stained by a wide band of dampness which reveals its abandonment; but in the air I breathed in there, I seemed to feel the sacred and pure breath of a glorious past.

"Ah," I thought. "What sublime aspirations, what heroic purposes were brought into this hall by the illustrious men who gathered here, to declare the liberty of a world!"

How distant they were from foreseeing the terrible waves of iniquities which would inundate the nation over and over again, in the aftermath of that legislation which they signed into being on that day, filled with idealistic hopes for the new world they were establishing for their children.

If those venerated heroes could raise the stone lids of their tombs today, they would find their splendid dreams realized, at least on Argentine soil. Liberty, justice, order, wealth, progress, and immense well-being, from the palace down to the humblest cabin.

Sleep your blessed sleep in peace, great initiators of the grand idea that ferments in our spirit; the hour is not far off when we, the offspring of all the American nations, will rise up united by a single thought: to sweep aside the infamous few who want to tyrannize over us, corrupt us or exploit us. May we finally implement justice, and gather all of Latin America in one fraternal embrace, from the Gulf of Darien to the Straits of Magellan, to create *the grand and glorious nation* which your prophetic minds foresaw and foretold.

RETURN TO BOLIVIA

Although she had no thought of returning to Bolivia when she left her husband, Gorriti's two daughters from that marriage eventually moved to La Paz, and Gorriti went to visit them. She was there when Belzú was assassinated (March 28, 1865) and she claimed the body and led a huge funeral procession through the city. This selection describes her reactions just after she crossed the border from Peru into Bolivia: "La Paz: Pasado y Presente" [La Paz: Past and Present] from *El Mundo de los Recuerdos*, 115-118.

One day the winds of life carried me once again to Bolivia, that land of sweet and painful memories. How different I found it from the era when, with my soul in conflict, I left it bloodied by civil war, its roads deserted, its fields untilled and sown with corpses.

Upon arriving at Chiliyaya, the first stop in Bolivian territory, there, where an inhospitable desert used to extend in all directions, the traveler now finds a population made up of picturesque bungalows grouped around an elegant and comfortable hotel, visited daily by numerous transient visitors brought to this improvised port by the activities of commerce.

From there, a coach service takes travelers in a few hours, across plains populated by ranches, cultivated fields and livestock, to the attractive city built in a hidden valley at the bottom of a ravine, by the auriferous banks of the Chuquiapo.

A wide highway which snakes daringly between precipices has replaced the vertiginous path where the walker used to fear for his life, suspended above abysses, until reaching the first streets of La Paz.

*   *   *

From the top of the ridge which overlooks it, as a bird might fly, I beheld La Paz, a city marked by so many catastrophes. While my gaze was taking in the vast panorama of the city, my mind wandered, evoking some of the gruesome events in its terrible history.

What a lugubrious historical epic has taken place within this circle of mountain peaks, from Tupac Amaru's siege to the battle over Melgarejo's barricades!

Just over here is the Alto de Santa Bárbara, where the Cacique de Guarina, betrayed by a traitor, was sacrificed!...

And here, where nowadays a marble fountain sends up its elegant spray, is where the prison stood in which the illustrious Murillo perished, passing on the inextinguishable torch of liberty as his legacy to the American world.

From these very windows, the bloodied corpses of Spaniards, from Governor Valdehoyos down to every single Spanish sympathizer living in the city, were hurled into the afternoon breeze by popular vengeance, implementing its cruel justice.

There stood the gallows of the terrible Ricafort; and there the gallows where so many renegade Americans hung their brothers, who were patriots. And there the fratricidal slaughters of the civil war. And over there.... The sound of happy exclamations reached me, and changed the course of my thoughts.

In the center of this very same plaza, site of so many horrors over the years, a military parade was now assembling itself, prelude of the holidays with which Bolivia celebrates its incorporation into the life of nations.

Beloved land, which adopted me lovingly the day when, stateless and homeless, I crossed your borders with a group of exiles:

May you be ever blessed and glorified!

MIRAFLORES, PERU

Gorriti wrote dozens of affectionate memoirs of her years in
Peru. When the Spanish besieged Callao, Peru in 1866, Gorriti
became a heroine of the Peruvian resistance, repeatedly risking
her life to save the wounded. She was awarded the Peruvian government's highest decoration for military valor, the "Estrella del
2 de mayo." This selection describes the town (now Lima suburb) of Miraflores before and after the invasion. "Miraflores"
from *El mundo de los recuerdos*, 343-348.

Shaded, fresh and perfumed, that oasis enclosed a double
enchantment. It bewitched the eyes with its magnificent palaces,
its flower gardens, its background of blue hills and skies. And
it lingered in memory, with its name: Miraflores [Behold the
Flowers]!

That was the name, too, of that beloved region where I was
born and which cradled my first days of life, eternal mirage of
the soul....

I remember the intense eagerness with which I awaited the
departure of the train each Saturday, when the week's work was
done. On wings of steam, it would carry us to that delicious
resort where we would enjoy the fresh air of country fields, the
perfume of the flowers, the embraces of the family.

White banners were waving in the breeze, greeting us, as the
station came into view from the train; and a whole throng of
glorious young people, representing the flowering ages of life,
were grouped all along the platform, waiting impatiently for the
travelers to step down. Sweet voices exclaimed delightedly.

Fathers and daughters, brothers and sisters, and courting cou-
ples, their fingers interlocked after a whole week apart—a centu-

ry!—conversing eagerly, strolled down the avenue of poplars that connects the station with the town....

And the happy crowd scattered into the flowery groves, into the gardens and parks, past tall green hedges, heading toward the sumptuous homes where hospitable banquets awaited them, served in elegant dining rooms or by the seaside, with places set on tablecloths spread out on the fresh grass beside barbecue pits where the succulent *pachamanca* is roasting.

And in the evening, there was a band concert in the town plaza in the moonlight; and on the balconies of the buildings that face onto the plaza, young people, with their arms around each other, danced to the *Habaneras* the musicians tackled bravely, while older people, back in the sitting rooms, enjoyed the pleasures of checkers, chess, backgammon and cards.

And the next day, Sunday morning, the joyful pealing of the bells again assembled the happy travelers, who gathered in the attractive church set between two gardens. White and well-kept, it was decorated everywhere with offerings of feminine piety, and was presided over by the beautiful image of the Virgin, who, from above the altar, extended her arms, smiling her celestial smile which filled the hearts of worshipers with peace.

And as they prayed, never has human devotion risen more fervently and purely to the throne of the Eternal than these sweet feminine prayers, in this rustic temple which their faith had filled with worthy gifts.

And leaving the temple, their beautiful faces still bathed in mystic reflections, they ran off—joyfully, singing, laughing—on happy excursions which would take them to gardens and bathing pools, to the ruins of the Viceroys' Palace and to the great library of the poet Palma, a resident there, who had one of the richest collections in Peru, definitely Peru's most interesting library in terms of its rare treasures.

But oh, these girls laughed and sang at the very edge of an abyss!

* * *

One day, the sea was covered with enemy ships.

Invading armies profaned the Peruvian soil, and leaving a trail of blood and fire through the coastal towns, they approached Lima and looked with greedy eyes at the rich metropolis.

The defending armies arranged themselves in a series of trenches along the outskirts of the town of Miraflores, where, when a truce was broken by traitorous deception, they fought like brave men and died like heroes...

Iberico, La Jana, Colina, Pignateli, Lavalle, Sánchez, Pino, Barron, Gómaz, Alfaro, and so many others: May you rest in your tombs in eternal peace!

The victorious enemy rushed hungrily into the beautifuil town and pillaged it; they fought over its treasures, and then set fire to the city.

The flames of the immense fire lit up the sky of the entire region that night.

* * *

A few days after the catastrophe that was decisive for the destiny of Peru, a feeling of nostalgia led me to make a pilgrimage to that place held so dear in memory.

It was a pile of rubble.

There were not even ashes left where Palma's library had stood: the wind had swept them away.

The poetic church, its doors smashed, stood there open to the elements, scorched, ransacked.

The whole town of elegant houses, parks and gardens was reduced to heaps of charred debris and remnants of beams and walls.

But, as if to be true to its name, *Miraflores*, Behold the Flowers, among the tumbled walls, vines had sprouted and bright patches of flowers bloomed: roses, jasmine, and honeysuckle, and there they were, opening their perfumed blossoms to the morning sun.

Introduction and translations by Mary G. Berg.

TRAVELS THROUGH PERU

Flora Tristán

Among the women included in this volume, Flora Tristán is
one of the best known international writers and feminists. Her
autobiographical travel journal, *Peregrinations of a Pariah* published in 1838, has received notable attention for its sense of
myth and political meaning. An ardent socialist, Tristán's
accounts in this anthology explore her travels to Peru disguised
as a *demoiselle*, a single woman, leaving behind an abusive husband and two children in Bordeaux, France.

Throughout her journeys, Tristán was able to observe the
Peruvian sites normally off limits to women, such as slave quarters and army barracks, as well as experience the upperclass life
in Peru. Her journal details how difficult it was to get past the
issues of social and gender inequality during the civil unrest and

war that broke out as she traveled both on land and on sea.

With her exposing journals, and feminist social criticism of the ways of life in Peru, Tristán did not realize the effect that her writings would have on others. After her journals were published, her Peruvian relatives expressed hatred for her, while her abusive husband tried to murder her, but fortunately she survived the unremovable bullet that he shot into her chest.

After her endeavors with her first text, Tristán wrote another travel narrative, *Promenade dans Londres,* published in 1840. This too, had detailed social criticism on the terrible living conditions in London at the time, but she does not reveal any secret particulars of history as she did in *Peregrinations of a Pariah.*

Tristán's text, *Peregrinations of a Pariah* sold out and went into a second edition, leaving an incredible impression on the Peruvians and the way of life during the 1800s. Although this book was written in French, Flora Tristán is a lasting influence in the Peruvian society. Like Juana Manuela Gorriti, Tristán represents the emergence of women into the international scene.

ON BOARD THE MEXICAIN

April 7th 1833, the anniversary of my birth, was the day of our departure. As the moment drew closer I felt so agitated that for three nights I was unable to enjoy a single hour of sleep. My body was broken, nevertheless I rose at daybreak so that I would have time to finish all my preparations, and this occupation calmed my mind. M Bertera came for me at seven o'clock and we went to the steamboat with the rest of my baggage. What a flock of unruly thoughts beset me on the brief journey to the port! The growing noise in the streets heralded a return to the bustle of daily life, and I leaned out of the cab in my eagerness to look again at the beautiful city where I had once spent so many tranquil days. The warm breeze touched my face;

I felt an overwhelming sense of life, yet grief and despair filled my soul. Like a condemned man being taken to his death, I envied the lot of the country women coming into town to sell their milk, the men going to work. We passed the city park, and I bade farewell to its lovely trees, recalling with feelings of profound regret the times I had walked beneath their shade. When we reached the steamboat the sight of all the people saying goodbye to their friends or making their way towards the surrounding countryside only increased my distress. God only knows how I overcame the impulse to say to M Bertera: "In heaven's name, save me! For pity's sake, take me away from here!" But the presence of so many people served as a grim reminder of the society that had banished me from its midst. At the memory my tongue froze and my body broke out in a cold sweat.

The signal was given to depart, the visitors went ashore and the boat began to draw away. I stayed below while the other passengers stood on deck waving their last farewells. Suddenly indignation gave me strength, and darting to one of the windows I cried in a voice choked with emotion: "You fools! I pity you, I cannot hate you. Your disdain hurts me, but my conscience is clear. I am the victim of the very laws and prejudices which make your own lives so bitter, but which you lack the courage to resist. If this is how you treat those whose lofty souls and generous hearts lead them to champion your cause, I warn you that you will remain wretched for many years to come."

This outburst restored my spirits and I began to feel calmer. The gentlemen of the *Mexicain* resumed to the saloon. Only M Chabrié seemed moved: his eyes were full of tears. My sympathetic look drew him towards me and he said: "It takes courage to leave one's country and one's friends, mademoiselle, but I hope we shall see them again...."

By the time we reached Pauillac I appeared resigned to my fate. I spent the night in writing my last letters, and the following day at about eleven o'clock I went on board the *Mexicain*.

The *Mexicain* was a new brig of about 200 tons and looked from her lines as if she would do well under sail. Accommodation on board was comfortable enough but very limited: the living space was sixteen or seventeen feet by twelve and contained four very small cabins, with a larger one for the captain at the far end. The first mate's cabin was just outside the entrance. The deck, encumbered with hencoops, baskets, and stores of every description, allowed only a restricted space for movement. The vessel was the joint property of M Chabrié, the captain, M Briet, the first mate, and M David, the second. They owned most of the cargo as well. There was a crew of fifteen: eight seamen, a carpenter, a cook, a cabin-boy, a boatswain and the three officers. All were young, strong, and perfectly competent, with the exception of the cabin-boy, whose laziness and dirtiness were a source of constant irritation. The ship was amply stocked with provisions and the cook was excellent.

There were only four other passengers: an elderly gentleman called Don José who had wanted to see his native Spain again before he died and was now on his way back to Peru, accompanied by his nephew Cesario, a remarkably intelligent youth of fifteen. The third passenger, Firmin Miota, was a Peruvian born in Cuzco, the city of the Sun. He had been sent to Paris at the age of sixteen to complete his education, and was now twenty-four. He was accompanied by his cousin Fernando, a young Biscayan of seventeen. Of the four, only M Miota spoke French.

The captain, M Zacharie Chabrié, was a man of thirty-six, born in Lorient, and quite unlike the usual captain in the merchant fleet. He had an abundance of natural wit and an astonishing gift for repartee, but what was most remarkable about him was the goodness of his heart and the loftiness of his imagination. His temper, on the other hand, was quite the worst I have ever encountered: he was so intolerably touchy that every little thing upset him, and when he was in a bad humour he was incapable of moderation.

At first sight M Chabrié appeared very ordinary, but one had only to speak to him for a few moments to realise how cultivated he was. He was of medium height, and must have been a fine figure of a man before he began to put on weight. He was almost bald, and the top of his head was so white that it made an odd contrast with his face, which was dark red. The sea had ruined his eyesight, but his little blue eyes sparkled with a blend of malice, effrontery and tenderness difficult to define. Everything about him was contradictory, including his voice. When he spoke it was impossible to imagine a more discordant sound, but when he sang a Rossini aria, a Tyrolean folk song or a sentimental ballad, it was like being lifted up to heaven. To complete the picture, I should add that he was very particular about his dress. He was sensitive to the cold, and from the moment he felt the first twinges of rheumatism in his legs, he began to take the greatest care of his health, protecting himself against cold and damp with an assortment of garments piled one on top of the other in the most ludicrous fashion.

The first mate, M Louis Briet, also came from Lorient and was the same age as M Chabrié. He had been a member of the Imperial Guards in 1815, but the fall of the Emperor cheated him of his hopes of glory, so he became a sailor, took his master's ticket, and went to try his fortune in the Spanish colonies. By nature he remained more of a soldier than a sailor, as unlike sailors he was a stickler for order. As well as being neat and efficient in everything he did, he was a man of the strictest sobriety.

M Briet was a very handsome man, tall and well made, with good features and a distinguished countenance. It was not in his nature to be attentive, let alone gallant, towards ladies; but on board his manner towards everybody was always very polite and perfecdy proper.

M Alfred David was thirty-four and typical of the Parisian who has seen the world. When he left the *College Bonaparte* at the age of fourteen, his parents sent him to sea aboard a merchantman bound for India to give him a taste of hardship. By the time they reached Calcutta the captain had had enough of this awkward customer and left him ashore, whereupon the lad boldly determined to earn his living, which he did. In turn sailor, language teacher, clerk, etc., he remained in India for five years. Back in France, he sought to settle down, but finding that he could not rely on the fine promises which are never lacking in Paris, he decided to try his luck once more in trade, and went off to Peru. In Lima he joined forces with M Chabrié and the two of them returned to France in 1832: M David had been away for eight years.

M David was self-taught, and while he had no profound knowledge of anything, he was acquainted with a variety of subjects. As he was left poor and helpless at a tender age, he learned about the human heart in a good school and his early disappointments destroyed his illusions. He hated the human race: he looked on men as wild animals and was always on his guard lest they should attack him. The poor man had never loved anyone, not even a woman: the gentle emotions of the soul were stifled in him before they had a chance to develop. He was passionately fond of good cheer, enjoyed smoking cigars, and delighted in thinking about the pretty girls of any colour he would meet in the next port of call. That was the only kind of love he understood.

M David was extremely good-looking, tall and very slim, but strong and healthy nevertheless. His delicate regular features, pale complexion, black side-whiskers, jet-black hair and the smile forever playing upon his lips combined to create an impression of cheerfulness very much at odds with his real feelings. M David was what people call an agreeable man. He was also a dandy who went round Cape Horn in silk stockings, trimmed his beard every day, scented his hair, recited poetry, spoke English, Italian and Spanish, and never lost his balance however much the ship was rolling.

Such were my companions on the *Mexicain*. From the moment we set foot on board, each of us was busy settling into his own little space as best he could. M David helped me arrange my things, and with his experience of sea voyages he was able to show me how to make myself as comfortable as possible.

I was seasick an hour after I came aboard my floating home. I shall spare my reader the tedium of yet another description of this affliction, except to say that it is quite unlike any of our common illnesses: it is a permanent agony, a suspension of life. Persons of an emotional nature feel its cruel effects more intensely than others do. As for me, I suffered from it so consistently that not one of the one hundred and thirty-three days of the voyage passed without an attack of nausea.

Our vessel was moored at the mouth of the river. The weather did not seem to favour our braving the perils of the Bay of Biscay, nevertheless at about three o'clock the captain gave orders to raise the anchor, and the ponderous machine, light as a feather on the waves, began to move across the immense expanse of water bounded by the sky. Hardly were we in the Bay than the shrill whistling of the winds and the tumult of the waves announced the impending storm which broke soon afterwards in all its fury. This was a new experience for me: I felt it though I did not see it. I would have found it fascinating to watch if I had had the strength, but all my faculties were absorbed by my sickness; I knew I was still alive only by the shivers that shook my body and seemed to presage my death. We had a dreadful night. The captain was lucky to be able to get back into the river. One wave had carried off our sheep, another our baskets of vegetables, and our poor little ship, so neat and trim the day before, was already crippled. The captain, though dropping with fatigue, went ashore to buy fresh sheep and replace the vegetables the sea had stolen from us. During his absence the carpenter repaired the ravages caused by the storm and the crew restored the order so necessary on board ship.

This first attempt did not make us any wiser, and we knowingly exposed ourselves a second time to dangers which very nearly claimed our lives, thanks to a false notion of honour, which all too often makes sailors brave unnecessary hazards and endanger the lives of men and the safety of vessels entrusted to their charge. The next day, April 10th, as the sea continued rough, our officers, who were very prudent, judged quite rightly that they ought to keep the pilot aboard until the weather improved sufficiently to send him back safely; but there were two other vessels moored close by, the *Charles Adolphe* and the *Flétès*, which had left Bordeaux at the same time and were bound for the same destination. The latter, out of bravado no doubt, sent back her pilot and made for the open sea; the other, not wishing to be left behind, did the same. Our gentlemen of the *Mexicain* began by blaming the foolhardiness of the other two ships, but although they were not the sort to let themselves be influenced by the example of others, the fear of being thought cowards made them abandon their earlier decision.

Towards four o'clock in the afternoon they sent back their pilot and we found ourselves amid the mountainous waves. We were nothing but a speck on the ocean, and if two waves had struck us at the same time, we would have been buried beneath them.

It was three days before we could struggle out of the Bay. We were constantly battered by the storm and our situation was critical. During those three long days of agony our brave captain never left the deck; he told me afterwards that several times he had seen our brig in imminent danger of being dashed against the rocks or swallowed up by the waves. Thanks to God we came out if it alive. You would think that such dangers ought to make sailors more careful, but no, they commit similar reckless acts every day.

Between two and three o'clock on the afternoon of the 13th, our captain, looking absolutely exhausted and as wet as if he had fallen into the sea, came below for the first time in three days. Seeing all the cabins closed and hearing no sound of life, he shouted in his hoarse voice: "Hello there! Passengers! Is everybody dead down here?"

Nobody answered his kind enquiry. Then M Chabrié half-opened my door and said with a solicitude I shall never forget: "Mademoiselle Flora, you have been very ill, so David tells me: poor young lady, I am really sorry for you as I used to suffer from seasickness myself, but take heart, we are out of the Bay at last and have come into the open sea—can't you feel it from the gentle rocking motion, so unlike the horrible convulsions we felt before? The weather is magnificent; if you felt strong enough to get up and come on deck, it would put new life into you. The air is so fresh and pure up there it's a pleasure to feel it."

I thanked him with a look, as I felt too weak even to attempt to speak.

"Poor young lady!" he repeated with an expression of kindness and compassion. "This weather will allow you to sleep. I am going to sleep too: I need it."

In fact we all slept a full twenty-four hours. I was awakened by M David opening all the cabin doors because he wanted to know, or so he said, if all the passengers were definitely dead. We were not dead, but dear God, what a state we were in! M Chabrié, who was above trading on his position of authority and spoke to his crew and passengers alike as a friend, now invited us to get up, so that we could change our linen, take the air on deck, and—most important of all—drink a little hot broth. For my part, I consented, on condition that I was excused from eating anything. The gentlemen were good enough to make me up a bed on deck, but it took me all my courage to get up and dress, and without their help it would have been impossible for me to climb on deck.

For the first fortnight of the voyage I felt quite numb, apart from brief intervals when I was conscious of my existence. From sunrise until about six in the evening I was so ill that I was unable to put two ideas together. I was indifferent to everything: my only desire was that death would come quickly and put an end to my sufferings—but an inner voice told me that I was not going to die.

Translated by Jean Hawkes.

TRAVELS THROUGH MEXICO

Frances Calderón de la Barca

Scottish by birth, American by upbringing, and Spanish by marriage, Frances Erskine Inglis Calderón de la Barca (1804-1882) experienced the world in many different ways as a woman, travelling with her husband in Mexico during the nineteenth century.

Calderón de la Barca journeyed to Mexico in 1839 with her husband, the first Spanish Minister to the recently-liberated Mexico. By 1842 Calderón de la Barca published *Life in Mexico*, where she recorded and exposed the unstable life in the land of Mexico. Her text offers insight on the political and social uprisings and violence that were present due to the political, religious, and social tensions in Mexico. Calderón de la Barca also wrote *Sketches of the Court of Isabella II* anonymously in 1856.

Writing through the eyes of a well-educated, upper-class white woman, Calderón de la Barca was moved by the Mexican culture and the daily instability that affected the entire society and its surroundings. Through her texts, she became known for her knowledge on Mexico during a completely devastating time. Calderón de la Barca's experiences in Mexico left a life-long impression on her and on her overall social, political, and religious views.

Sunday: October 27th, 1839
On board the Packet Ship Norma

This morning at ten o'clock we left New York and stepped on board the steamboat *Hercules*, destined to convey us to our packet with its musical name. The day was foggy and gloomy, as if refusing to be comforted, even by an occasional smile from the sun. All prognosticated that the *Norma* would not sail today, but all were mistaken—"where there's a will, there's a way."

Several of our friends had come to see us off and accompanied us to the wharf: Bodisco, the Russian minister, who is about taking a part in El Sí de las Niñas; Mr. Krehmer, who tried hard to look sentimental, and even brought tears into his eyes by some curious process he must have learned in St. Petersburg—"The tear forgot as soon as shed"; Judge Patterson; Mariquita Harmony; Suárez, who looked like a stale lemon; Trueman, who appeared on the scene to increase the effect at the last moment; also General Alvear, the minister of Buenos Aires,&c., &c.

Richmond, A. Norman, Jane, and Mary Jones, from whom we were truly sorry to part, accompanied us as far as the ship. The *Norma* was anchored in one of the most beautiful points of the bay—and, luggage hoisted in, the steamboat towed us five miles, until we had passed the Narrows. The wind was contrary, but the day began to clear up, and the sun to scatter the watery clouds. Stoughton came in a boat, and made the amiable. His motto is, "Welcome the coming, speed the parting guest."

Still, there is nothing so sad as a retreating view. It is as if time were visibly in motion; and as here we had to part from [my family] we could only distinguish, as through a misty veil, the beauties of the bay; the shores covered to the water's edge with trees rich in their autumnal colouring; the white houses on Staten Island—the whole gradually growing fainter till, like a dream, they faded away.

The pilot has left us, breaking our last link with the land. We still see the mountains of Navesink, and the lighthouse of Sandy Hook. The sun is setting, and in a few minutes we must take our leave, probably for years, of places long familiar to us. We have said adieu to Richmond, and Jane, and A. Norman, and Mary Jones—and Spanish-Yankee Stoughton—and Zaldo, who makes fair promises. And now we are alone, Calderón and I and Mme Martin, my French *femme de chambre*, with her air of offended dowager duchess, and moreover seasick.

Our fellow passengers do not appear very remarkable. There is Madame Albini—returning from being prima donna in Mexico, in a packet called after the opera in which she was there a favourite—with an awful looking man, her husband, Señor Vellani, with moustaches like a bird's nest, and a baby and nurse, a Mme de Roy, a pretty widow in deep affliction, at least in deep mourning, of whom more anon; an old maiden lady, Miss Fay, going out as a governess, under our protection they say; a family whose names I do not know; and every variety of ugly Spaniard, from Bird's Nest Vellani to an old

Habañero consul, going out to replace the disgraced Trist.

Monday evening: October 28th, 1839

When I said I liked a sea life, I did not mean to be understood as liking a nasty dirty merchant ship, full of vulgar Spaniards who smoke and spit worse than the most be-Trolloped Americans. I did not mean that I liked a cabin without air, and with every variety of bad smell—and no chance of a good one. As the Albini, with the air of an afflicted porpoise and with more truth than elegance expresses it: *"Tout devient puant, même l'eau de cologne!"*

The wind is still contrary and the *Norma*, beating up and down, makes but little way. The captain says we have not gone more than seventy-four miles, and of these advanced but forty. He, Captain Barton, has now made fifty-four voyages to and from Havana.

Nothing very remarkable has occurred today. Most people sick—passively or actively—and the deck is nearly deserted. The most interesting object I have yet discovered on board is a pretty little deaf and dumb girl, very lively and with an intelligent face, who has been trying to teach me to speak on my fingers. There is a large iron sugar machine on board, which looks enough to weigh down the vessel. Spent the day on deck, to avoid the purgatory of bad odours which pervades the cabin. Mme de Roy made her first appearance on deck—and gave a mortal blow to the interest with which her history had inspired me by her performance in public. It is said that her husband being at New York, and dying of consumption, she rejected every entreaty and advice that was given her to advise him to have his will made, saying that his last moments should not be disturbed—by which means, he dying without a will, she has been left destitute.

The only commendable part of the ship is the food, which is very decent indeed—but ah! the difference between this and a Liverpool or Havre packet! Charles Napoleon, the infant heir of the houses of Albini and Vellani, has shown his good taste by passing the day in screaming. Bird's Nest Vellani, pale, dirty, and much resembling a brigand out of employ, has traversed the deck with uneasy footsteps, and a cigar appearing from out his moustaches, like a light in a tangled forest, or a jack-o'-lantern in a marshy thicket. A horrid fat Spaniard has been discoursing on the glories of garlic and *olla podrida*. *Au reste*, we are slowly pursuing our way and if we go on at this rate might reach Cuba in three months.

And the stars are shining, quiet and silvery. All without is soft and beautiful, and no doubt the *Norma* herself with her white sails spread looks all in unison with the scene, balancing herself like a lazy swan, white and graciously. So it is without, and within there is miserable seasickness, bilge water, bad smells, fat Spaniards, and Bird's Nest Vellani!—and all the unavoidable disagreeables of a small packet.

* * *

Holy Week

On the morning of Palm Sunday I went to the cathedral, accompanied; Mademoiselle de Cyprey, daughter of the French minister. We found it no easy matter to make our way through the crowd, but at last, by dint of patience and perseverance, and changing our place very often, we contrived to arrive very near the great altar. There we had just taken up our position when a disinterested man gave us a friendly hint that, as the whole procession, with their branches, must inevitably squeeze past the very spot where we were, we should probably be crushed or suffocated. Consequently we followed him to a more convenient station, also close to the altar and defended by the railing, where we found ourselves tolerably well off. Two ladies, to whom he made the same condition, and who rejected it, we afterwards observed in a sad condition, their *mantillas* nearly torn off and the palm branches sweeping across their eyes.

In a short time, the whole cathedral presented the appearance of a forest of palm trees *(à la* Birnam wood), moved by a gentle wind; and under each tree a half-naked Indian, his rags clinging together with wonderful pertinacity; long, matted, dirty black hair both in men and women, bronze faces and mild unspeaking eyes—or all with one expression of eagerness to see the approach of the priests. Many of them had probably travelled a long way, and the palms were from *tierra caliente,* dried and plaited into all manner of ingenious ways. Each palm was about seven feet high, so as far to overshadow the head of the Indian who carried it; and whenever they are blessed, they are carried home to adorn the walls of their huts. The priests arrived at length, in great pomp and also carrying palm branches. For four mortal hours we remained kneeling or sitting on the floor, and thankful we were when it was all over and we could make our way once more into the fresh air.

From this day, during the whole week, all business is suspended, and but one train of thought occupies all classes, from the highest to the lowest. The peasants flock from every quarter, shops are shut, churches are opened; and the Divine Tragedy enacted in Syria eighteen hundred years ago is now celebrated in land then undiscovered, and by the descendants of nations sunk in paganism for centuries after that period.

But amongst the lower classes the worship is emphatically the worship of her who herself predicted, "From henceforth all nations shall call me blessed." Before her shrines, and at all hours, thousands are kneeling. With faces expressive of the most intense love and devotion, and with words of the most passionate adoration, they address the mild image of the Mother of God. To the Son their feelings seem composed of respectful pity, of humble but more distant adoration; while to the Virgin they appear to give all their confidence, and to look up to her as to a kind and bountiful queen, who—dressed in her magnificent robes and jewelled diadem, yet mourning in all the agony of her divine sorrows—has condescended to admit the poorest beggar to participate in her woe, whilst in her turn she shares in the afflictions of the lowly, feels for their privations, and grants them her all-powerful intercession.

On Holy Thursday nothing can be more picturesque than the whole appearance of Mexico. No carriages are permitted and the ladies, being on foot, take the opportunity of displaying all the riches of their toilet. On this day velvets and satins are your only wear. Diamonds and pearls walk the streets. The *mantillas* are white or black blonde; the shoes white or coloured satin. The petticoats are still rather short, but it would be hard to hide such small feet, and such still smaller shoes. "*Il faut souffrir pour être belle,*" but *a quoi bon être belle?* if no one sees it. As for me I ventured upon a lilac silk of Palmyre's, and a black *mantilla*.

The whole city was filled with picturesque figures. After the higher señoras were to be remarked the common women, chiefly in clear white very stiffly starched muslins—some very richly embroidered, and the petticoat trimmed with lace—white satin shoes, and the dresses extremely short, which on them looks very well. A *rebozo* is thrown over all. Amongst these there were many handsome faces, but in a still lower and more Indian class, with their gay-coloured petticoats, the faces were sometimes beautiful, and the figures more upright and graceful; also they invariably walk well, whilst many of the higher classes, from tight shoes and want of custom, seem to feel pain in putting their feet to the ground.

But none could vie with the handsome Poblana peasants in their holiday dresses, some so rich and magnificent that, remembering the warning of our ministerial friends, I am inclined to believe them more showy than respectable. The pure Indians, with whom the churches and the whole city is crowded, are as ugly as can be imagined: a gentle, dirty, and much-enduring race. Still, with their babies at their backs, going along at their usual gentle trot, they add much to the general effect of the *coup-d'oeil*.

We walked to San Francisco about ten o'clock, and, the body of the church being crowded, went upstairs to a private gallery with a gilded grating belonging to the Countess de Santiago, and here we had the advantage of seats, besides a fine view of the whole. This church is very splendid, and the walls were hung with canvas paintings representing different passages of our Saviour's life (his entry into Jerusalem, the woman of Samaria at the well, &c.) which, with the palm trees, had a cool and oriental effect.

Before the altar, which was dazzling with jewels, was a representation of the Lord's Supper, not in painting, but in sculptured figures as large as life, habited in the Jewish dresses. The bishops and priests were in a blaze of gold and jewels. They were assisted during the ceremony by the young Count of Santiago. The music was extremely good, and the whole effect impressive.

We visited several churches in the course of the day, and continued walking until four o'clock, when we went to dine with our friends the Adalids. After dinner one of their coachmen, a handsome Mexican in a superb dress all embroidered in gold, was called upstairs to dance the *jarabe* to us with a country girl. The dance is monotonous, but they acquitted themselves to perfection.

We then continued our pilgrimage through the city, though, as the sun had not yet set, we reserved our chief admiration until the churches should be illuminated. One, however, we entered at sunset, which was worthy of remark: Santo Domingo. It looked like a little paradise, or a story in the Arabian Nights. All the steps up the altar were covered with pots of beautiful flowers, orange trees loaded with fruit and blossom, and rosebushes in full bloom, glasses of coloured water, and all kinds of fruit. Cages full of birds, singing delightfully, hung from the wall, and really fine paintings filled up the intervals. A gay carpet covered the floor, and in front of the altar, instead of the usual representation of the Saviour crucified, a little Infant Jesus, beautifully done in wax, was lying amidst flowers with little angels surrounding him. Add to this the music of *Romeo and Juliet* and you may imagine that it was more like a scene in an opera than anything in a church. But certainly, as the rays of the setting sun streamed with a rosy light through the stained windows, throwing a glow over the whole—birds, and flowers, and fruit, paintings and angels—it was the prettiest and most fantastic scene I ever beheld, like something expressly got up for the benefit of children.

We did not kneel before each altar for more than three minutes, otherwise we should never have had time even to enter the innumerable churches which we visited in the course of the night. We next went to Santa Teresa la Nueva, a handsome church belonging to a convent of strict nuns; which was now brilliantly illuminated, and here, as in all the churches, we made our way through the crowd with extreme difficulty. The number of *léperos* was astonishing, greatly exceeding that of well-dressed people. Before each altar was a figure, dreadful in the extreme, of the Saviour as large as life, dressed in purple robe and crown of thorns, seated on the steps of the altar, the blood trickling from his wounds, each person, before leaving the church, devoutly kneeling to kiss his hands and feet. The nuns, amongst whom is a sister of Señor Adalid, sung behind the grating in the gallery above, but were not visible.

One of the churches we visited, that of Santa Teresa called the *Antigua*, stands upon the site formerly occupied by the palace of the father of the unfortunate Montezuma. It was here that the Spaniards were quartered when they took Montezuma prisoner, and here Cortés found and appropriated the treasures of that family. In 1830 a bust of stone was found in the yard of the convent, which the workmen were digging up. Don Lucas Alamán, then Minister of Exterior Relations, offered a compensation to the nuns for the curious piece of antiquity, which they gladly gave up to the government on whose account he acted. It is said to be the idol goddess of the Indians, Centeotl, the goddess of medicine and medicinal herbs, also known by the name of Temazcalteci, or the "Grandmother of the Baths." A full account is given of her in one of the numbers of the *Mosaico Mexicano*, as also of a square stone found in the same place, beautifully carved and covered with hieroglyphical characters.

In the evening, towards the hour when the great procession

was expected, we went to the balconies of the Academia, which command a fine view of the streets by which it was to pass. Till it arrived we amused ourselves by looking over the *beaux restes* of former days, the collections of painting and sculpture; the fine plaster-casts that still remain, and the great volumes of fine engravings. It was dark when the procession made its appearance, which rendered the effect less gaudy and more striking. The Virgin, the saints, the Holy Trinity, the Saviour in different passages of his life, imprisonment and crucifixion were carried past in succession, represented by figures magnificently dressed, placed on lofty scaffoldings of immense weight, supported by different bodies of men. One is carried by the coachmen, another by the *aguadores* (water carriers), a third by the *cargadores* (porters), a Herculean race.

First arrived the favourite protectress of all classes, the Virgin of Dolores, surmounted by a velvet canopy, seated on a glittering throne, attired in her sable robes, her brow surmounted by glittering rays and contracted with an expression of agony; of all representations of the Virgin, the only one which is always lovely, however rudely carved, with that invariably beautiful face of terrible anguish. Then followed the Saviour bearing the cross; the Saviour crucified, the Virgin supporting the head of her dying son; the Trinity (the Holy Spirit represented by a dove); all the apostles, from St. Peter with the keys to Judas with the moneybag; and a long train of saints, all brilliantly illuminated and attended by an amazing crowd of priests, monks, and laymen. However childish and superstitious all this may seem, I doubt whether it be not as well thus to impress certain religious truths on the minds of a people too ignorant to understand them by any other process. By the time the last saint and angel had vanished, the hour was advanced, and we had still to visit the illuminated churches. Being recommended to divest ourselves of our ornaments before wandering forth amongst the crowd, a matter of some moment to the Señora Adalid who wore all her diamonds, we left our earrings, brooches, &c., in charge of the person who keeps the Academia, and recommenced our pilgrimage.

Innumerable were the churches we visited that evening: the cathedral, La Enseñanza, Jesus María, Santa Clara, Santa Brígida, San Hipólito, La Encarnación, the five churches of San Francisco, &c., &c., a list without an end—kneeling for a short space of time before each blazing altar, for the more churches one visits, the more meritorious is the devotions.

The cathedral was the first we entered, and its magnificence struck us with amazement. Its gold and silver and jewels, its innumerable ornaments and holy vessels, the rich dresses of the priests, all seemed burning in almost intolerable brightness. The high altar was the most magnificent; the second, with its pure white marble pillars, the most imposing.

The crowd was immense, but we made our way slowly through it to the foot of each altar, where the people were devoutly kissing the Saviour's hand or the hem of his garment; or beating their breasts before the mild image of Our Lady of Grief. Each church had vied with the other in putting forth all its splendour of jewelry, of lights, of dresses, and of music.

In the church of Santa Clara—attached to the convent of the same name, small but elegant, with its pillars of white marble and gold—one voice of angelic sweetness was singing behind the grating alone, and in the midst of a most deathlike stillness. It sounded like the notes of a nightingale in a cage. I could have listened for hours, but our time was limited and we set off anew. Fortunately the evening was delightful, and the moon shining brightly. We visited about twenty churches in succession. In all the organ was pealing, the blaze of light overpowering, the magnificence of jewels and crimson velvet and silver and gold dazzling, the crowd suffocating, the incense blinding.

The prettiest effect in every church was caused by the orange trees and rosebushes, which covered the steps of the altars up to where the magnificence of the altar itself blazed out; and the most picturesque effect was produced by the different orders of monks in their gowns and hoods, either lying on their faces or standing ranged with torches like figures carved in stone.

In the passage leading to most of the churches was a table, at which several ladies of the highest rank sat collecting alms for the poor. The fair *quêteuses* had not been very successful, and that chiefly amongst the lower classes. The fatigue was terrible, walking for so many hours on that bad pavement with thin satin shoes, so that at length our feet seemed to move mechanically—and we dropped on our knees before each altar like machines touched by a spring, and rose again with no small effort.

Of all the churches we entered that night, the cathedral was the most magnificent, but the most beautiful and tasteful was San Francisco. The crowd there was so dense that we were almost carried off our feet, and were obliged, in defiance of all rule, to take the arms of our *caballeros*. Still, it was worth the trouble of making our way through it to see such a superbly illuminated altar. It was now eleven o'clock, and the crowd was breaking up as the churches are shut before midnight. On one corner of the middle aisle, near the door, was the representation of a prison from which issued a stream of soft music, and at the window was a figure of Christ in chains, his eyes bandaged and a Jew on each side; the chains hanging from his hands, and clanking as if with the motion of his arms. The rush here was immense. Numbers of people were kneeling before the window of the prison, and kissing the chains and beating their breasts with every appearance of contrition and devotion. This was the night before the Crucifixion, and the last scene of the Holy Thursday.

We reached home hardly able to stand. I never felt more dazzled, bewildered, and sleepy; but I was awakened by finding a packet of letters from home, which brought back my thoughts— rather carried them away to very different lands.

On Good Friday, a day of sorrow and humiliation, the scene in the morning is very different. The great sacrifice is complete— the Immortal has died a mortal death. The ladies all issue forth in mourning, and the churches look sad and wan after their last night's brilliancy. The heat was intense. We went to San Francisco, again to the *tribuna* of the Countess de Santiago, to see the Adoration and Procession of the Cross, which was very fine.

But the most beautiful and original scene was presented towards sunset in the great square, and it is doubtful whether any other city in the world could present a *coup d'oeil* of equal brilliancy. Having been offered the *entrée* to some apartments in the palace, we took our seats on the balconies, which commanded a view of the whole. The plaza itself, even on ordinary days, is a noble square, and but for its one fault—a row of shops called the Parián, which breaks its uniformity—would be nearly unrivalled. Every object is interesting. The eye wanders from the cathedral to the house of Cortés (the Monte Pío), and from thence to a range of fine buildings with lofty arcades to the west. From our elevated situation, we could see all the different streets that branch out from the square covered with gay crowds pouring in that direction to see another great procession, which was expected to pass in front of the palace. Booths filled with refreshments, and covered with green branches and garlands of flowers, were to be seen in all directions, surrounded by a crowd who were quenching their thirst with *orgeat, chía,* lemonade, or *pulque.*

The whole square, from the cathedral to the *portales* and from the Monte Pío to the palace, was covered with thousands and tens of thousands of figures, all in their gayest dresses, and as the sun poured his rays down upon their gaudy colours they looked like armies of living tulips. Here was to be seen a group of ladies, some with black gowns and mantillas; others, now that their churchgoing duty was over, equipped in velvet or satin, with their hair dressed—and beautiful hair they have; some leading their children by the hand, dressed—alas! how they were dressed! Long velvet gowns trimmed with blonde, diamond earrings, high French caps befurbelowed with lace and flowers, or turbans with plumes of feathers. Now and then the head of a little thing that could hardly waddle alone might have belonged to an English dowager duchess in her opera box. Some had extraordinary bonnets, also with flowers and feathers, and as they toddled along, top-heavy, one would have thought they were little old women—till a glimpse was caught of their lovely little brown faces and black eyes. Now and then a little girl, simply dressed with a short frock and long black hair plaited down and uncovered, would trip along, a very model of grace amongst the small caricatures. The children here are generally beautiful, their features only too perfect and regular for the face "to fulfill the promise of its spring." They have little colour, with swimming black or hazel eyes and long lashes resting on the clear pale cheek, and a perfect mass of fine dark hair of the straight Spanish or Indian kind plaited down behind.

As a contrast to the señoras, with their overdressed beauties, were the poor Indian women, trotting across the square, their black hair plaited with dirty red ribbon, a piece of woolen cloth wrapped round them, and a little mahogany baby hanging behind, its face upturned to the sky and its head going jerking along somehow without its neck being dislocated. The most resigned expression on earth is that of an Indian baby.

All the groups we had seen promenading the streets the day before were here collected by hundreds: the women of the shop-keeper class, or it may be lower, in their smart white embroidered gowns, with their white satin shoes, and neat feet and ankles, and *rebozos* or bright shawls thrown over their heads; the peasants and countrywomen, with their short petticoats of two colours, generally scarlet and yellow (for they are most anti-Quakerish in their attire), thin satin shoes and lace-trimmed chemises; or bronze-coloured damsels, all crowned with flowers, strolling along with their admirers, and tingling their light guitars. And above all, here and there a flashing Poblana, with a dress of real value and much taste, and often with a face and figure of extraordinary beauty, especially the figure—large, and yet *élancée,* with a bold coquettish eye, and a beautiful little brown foot shown off by the white satin shoe, the petticoat of her dress frequently fringed and embroidered in real massive gold, and either a *rebozo* shot with gold or a bright-coloured China crepe shawl coquettishly thrown over her head. We saw several whose dresses could not have cost less than five hundred dollars.

Add to this motley crowd, men dressed *á la Mexicaine,* with their large ornamented hats and serapes, or embroidered jackets, sauntering along smoking their cigars; *léperos* in rags;

Indians in blankets; officers in uniform; priests in their shovel hats; monks of every order; Frenchmen exercising their wit upon the passers-by; Englishmen looking cold and philosophical; Germans gazing through their spectacles, mild and mystical; Spaniards seeming pretty much at home, and abstaining from remarks—and it may be conceived that the scene at least presented variety. Sometimes the tinkling of the bell announced the approach of *Nuestro Amo*. Instantly the whole crowd are on their knees, crossing themselves devoutly. Two men who were fighting below the window suddenly dropped down side by side. Disputes were hushed, flirtations arrested, and to the busy hum of voices succeeded a profound silence. Only the rolling of the coach wheels and the sound of the little bell were heard.

No sooner had it passed than the talkers and the criers recommenced with fresh vigour. The venders of hot chestnuts and cooling beverages plied their trade more briskly than ever. A military band struck up an air from *Semiramis*; and the noise of the innumerable *matracas* (rattles), some of wood and some of silver, with which everyone is armed during the last days of the holy week, broke forth again as if by magic, while again commenced the sale of the Judases, fireworks in the form of that archtraitor which are sold on the evening of Good Friday and let off on Saturday morning.

Hundreds of these hideous figures were held above the crowd by men who carried them tied together on long poles. An ugly misshapen monster they represent the betrayer to have been. When he sold his Master for thirty pieces of silver, did he dream that in the lapse of ages his effigies should be held up to the execration of a Mexican mob, of an unknown people in undiscovered countries beyond the seas? A secret bargain, perhaps made whisperingly in a darkened chamber with the fierce Jewish rulers, but now shouted forth in the ears of the descendants of Montezuma and Cortés!

But the sound of a distant hymn rose on the air, and shortly after there appeared advancing towards the square a long and pompous retinue of mitred priests, with banners and crucifixes and gorgeous imagery, conducting a procession in which figures representing scenes concerning the death of our Saviour were carried by on platforms, as they were the preceding evening. There was the Virgin in mourning at the foot of the cross—the Virgin in glory—and more saints and more angels—St. Michael and the dragon, &c., &c.—a glittering and innumerable train. Not a sound was heard as the figures were carried slowly onwards in their splendid robes, lighted by thousands of tapers which mingled their unnatural glare with the fading light of day.

As the *Miserere* was to be performed in the cathedral late in the evening, we went there, though with small hopes of making our way through the tremendous crowd. Having at length been admitted through a private entrance, per favour, we made our way into the body of the church; but the crowd was so intolerable that we thought of abandoning our position, when we were seen and recognized by some of the priests and conducted to a railed-off enclosure near the shrine of the Virgin, with the luxury of a Turkey carpet. Here, separated from the crowd, we sat down in peace on the ground. The gentlemen were accommodated with high-backed chairs beside some ecclesiastics, for men may sit on chairs and benches in church, but women must kneel or sit on the ground. Why? "*Quién sabe?* Who knows?" is all the satisfaction I have ever obtained on that point.

The music began with a crash that awakened me out of an agreeable slumber into which I had gradually fallen; and such discordance of instruments and voices, such confusion worse confounded, such inharmonious harmony, never before deafened mortal ears. The very spheres seemed out of tune, and rolling and crashing over each other. I could have cried *Miserere!* with the loudest; and in the midst of all the undrilled band was a music master, with violin-stick uplifted, rushing desperately from one to the other, in vain endeavouring to keep time, and frightened at the clamour he himself had been instrumental in raising, like Phaeton entrusted with his unmanageable coursers. The noise was so great as to be really alarming, and the heat was severe in proportion. The calm face of the Virgin seemed to look reproachfully down. We were thankful when, at the conclusion of this stormy appeal for mercy, we were able to make our way into the fresh air and soft moonlight through the confusion and squeezing at the doors, where it was rumoured that a soldier had killed a baby with his bayonet. A bad place for poor little babies—decidedly.

Outside in the square it was cool and agreeable. A military band was playing airs from the *Norma*, and the womenkind were sitting on the stones of the railing, or wandering about and finishing their day's work by a quiet flirtation *au clair de la lune*.

It was now eleven o'clock, and the *pulquerías* were thrown open for the refreshment of the faithful, and though hitherto much order had prevailed it was not likely to endure much longer; notwithstanding which, we had the imprudence to walk unattended to our own house at San Fernando. In the centre of the city there seemed no danger. People were still walking, and a few still drinking at the lighted booths; but when we arrived at the lower part of the Alameda all was still, and as we walked outside under the long shadows of the trees I expected every moment to be attacked, and wished we were anywhere, even on the silvery top of Popocatepetl! We passed several crowded *pulquerías*, where some were drinking and others drunk. Arrived at the arches, we saw from time to time a suspicious blanketed figure half hid by the shadow of the wall. A few doors from our own domicile was a *pulque* shop filled with *léperos*, of whom some were standing at the door shrouded in their blankets. It seemed to me we should never pass them, but we walked fast and reached our door in safety. Here we thundered in vain. The porter was FEW and for nearly ten minutes we heard voices within, male and female, ineffectually endeavouring to persuade the heavy-headed Cerberus to relinquish his keys. It would have been a choice moment for our friends had any of them wished to accost us; but either they had not observed us, or perhaps they thought that Calderón, walking so late, must have been armed—or perhaps, more charitable construction, they had profited by the solemnities of the day.

We got in at last, and I felt thankful enough for shelter and safety, and as wearied of the day's performances as you may be in reading a description of them.

Next morning, *Sábado de Gloria*, I could not persuade myself to go as far as the plaza, to see the Iscariots explode. At a distance we listened to the hissing and crackling of the fireworks, the ringing of all the bells, and the thundering of artillery—and knew by the hum of busy voices, and the rolling of carriages, that the Holy Week was numbered with the past.

We hear that it is in contemplation amongst the English here, headed by their minister, to give a ball in the Minería to celebrate the marriage of Queen Victoria, which will be turning these splendid halls to some account.

I have some intention of giving a series of weekly soirées, but am assured that they will not succeed, because hitherto such parties have failed. As a reason is given the extravagant notions of the ladies in point of dress, and it is said that nothing but a ball where they can wear jewels and a toilet therewith consistent will please them; that a lady of high rank, who had been in Madrid, having proposed simple *tertulias* and white muslin dresses, half the men in Mexico were ruined that year by the embroidered French and India muslins bought by their wives during this reign of simplicity—the idea of a plain white muslin, a dress worn by any *lépera*, never having struck them as possible. Nevertheless we can but make the attempt.

We propose going next week to Tulancingo, where our friends the Adalids have a country place; from thence we proceed to visit the mines of Real del Monte.

Tuesday: April 23rd, 1840

On Monday we gave a *tertuilia* which, notwithstanding all predictions, went off remarkably well, and consisted of nearly all the pleasantest people in Mexico. We had music, dancing, and cards, and at three in the morning the German cotillion was still in full vigour. Everyone was disposed to be amused, and moreover the young ladies were dressed very simply, most of them in plain white muslins. There was but a small sprinkling of diamonds, and that chiefly among the elderly part of the community. Still, it is said that the novelty alone induced them to come, and that weekly soirées will not succeed. We shall try. Besides which, the lady of the French minister proposes being at home on Wednesday evenings; the lady of the Prussian minister takes another evening; I, a third, and we shall see what can be effected.

TRAVELS THROUGH CUBA

María de la Merced Beltrán

María de la Merced Beltrán de Santa Cruz y Montalvo, "The Countess of Merlin," (1789-1852) was born into privilege and aristocracy. She left Cuba at age twelve and moved to Paris, where she lived until her death.

In Paris, she held a well-respected literary salon where recitals and galas were common. Balzac, George Sand, and Morimeé were among the list of habitual and influential guests.

La Havane (1844), together with her memoirs, represents her most important work. In this extensive collection, written in the form of epistolary letters, Beltrán addresses childhood memories, her Creole heritage, and her European upbringing.

Day 7 at 8 in the morning
A few hours more and we are in Cuba. Amid so much activ-

ity, I remain here, immobile, breathing my native air, and in a state almost comparable with love itself.

You already know of my dislike of steamships, dislike that is heightened by the idea of the poetry of sailboats. Experience has confirmed my aversion to the former and preference for the latter. It is incontestable that the movement of a sailboat is smoother and more regular than the movement of a steamship. The latter, in addition to rocking and pitching, is beaten without end by the shaking caused by the movement of the wheels, without mentioning the violent and harsh jerking that is felt when it forcefully splits the agitated waves. I'm not even talking about the untidiness, the discomfort, and other disadvantages inseparable from the use of steam. The feelings of women aren't the domain of economists; for as admirable as is that man's intelligence puts the elements to work in order to take advantage of the result of their struggle, to me a man alone battling the elements seems grander. I love this combat more, this danger, this uncertainty about the future, with its excitements, its surprises, its joys. A sea voyage by sailboat is a poem full of beauty and of vicissitudes in which man appears in all of the greatness of his science and of his will, ennobling the danger by the calculated boldness with which he sweeps it away. To the whims or the furor of the sea, he matches his power and wisdom, his continual vigilance and his marvelous patience, and always in battle with the innumerable accidents of the elements, he knows equally to use them to their fullest and to dominate them.

Man has found the means to capture fire and calculate its effects. But winds are uncertain and their force unknown, their rage unforeseen, and this same uncertainty is what constitutes the poetry of sailboats. It is the human life with its uncertainties, its fears, its hopes, is false happinesses; and when good fortune arrives, when the good wind blows through the stern, oh! how he receives it, how he greets it, how he celebrates it, how it intoxicates the entire crew with its gust of life and hope.

You would be enchanted if you saw from the shore the grace and elegance of our boat, adorned with all its finery, the sails unfurled, the ropes perfectly tied, gliding hastily and merrily on the blue sea, like a young girl who is going to a dance.

A steamship travels more quickly; one knows ahead of time the day of arrival, to the point that one has the right, as with ground transportation, to impose a fine if one doesn't arrive at the scheduled time. I also know that there are those who find much beauty in steamships, that the aficionados are delighted by the view offered by the column of smoke dissipating in the air. To me, the smoke doesn't please me any more than that from a factory. And, as I'm never in such a hurry on my trips, I don't need to choose a steamship over a good carriage that doesn't go as far but as I wish. In a word, as I prefer my salon to my kitchen, I will leave the steamship to the merchants and their merchandise and will always travel by sail.

At midday I am seated in my chair. The sun vibrates its rays on my head, and I write to you on my lap...I am happy, and I want you to share in my happiness.

We are advancing with the beloved coast always before our eyes. A crowd of fishing boats passes from every side; they move away from and return to the shore. The ocean breeze that began two hours ago fills the sails of the boats that move toward the port's entrance. Some get ahead of us and we lose sight of them; others follow us or fight to pass us; and all are animated in their movement and magnificently lit by the beautiful sky. They appear in the air, and they are reflected in the surface of this serene and blue sea, while the waves, divided in every direction by a multitude of keels, rise proudly to then fall in plumes of foam with a type of voluptuousness, dragging after them thousands of fish of thousands of changing colors that glide, jump, and play in the water.

We can already make out the Pan de Matanzas, the highest of our mountains. At the peak is the city by that name, inhabited by two thousand souls and surrounded by sugar plantations. At some distance, and nearer to the coast, I find the village of Puerto Escondido. Upon seeing the cone-shaped cabanas, covered to the ground by palm leaves; upon seeing the brambles intertwined with banana trees that protect the houses from the heat of the sun with their large leaves; upon seeing the canoes tied to the shore; and upon contemplating the silent stillness of midday, it would seem that these beaches are still inhabited by Indians.

We have before us the city of Santa Cruz, which received its name from my ancestors, and that progresses graciously toward the shore. Its port serves as a shelter for the fishermen and as a market for the fruit of the neighboring towns. These small cities located at the edge of the sea don't have the right to export except to Havana, general warehouse of the island, that then scatters the goods to all regions of the globe.

What is that beautiful, picturesque city with a port so well protected from the hurricanes? It is the city of Jaruco, to which is tied my family's original title. My brother is chief judge of the city and, even more, he is its benefactor.

We are advancing rapidly. Castillo de la Fuerza is already behind us, with its two dismantled bastions and two garrison soldiers. In the times of Philip II, they tried for the first time to erect fortifications in his new overseas states, but the Royal Council decided there was no need, so great was the Spaniards' belief in their own strength. Nevertheless, pirates from all nations wasted no time in laying waste to the coasts of La

Española and Cuba. In 1538, Cuba was plundered, burned, and destroyed by a troop of filibusters, and its inhabitants had to take refuge in the woods.

The Governor don Hernando de Soto, who's had sovereign authority over the island, ordered that they rebuild the city and construct the Castillo de la Fuerza, which wasn't completed until 1544. Until then, ships and the Spanish fleet weren't allowed to enter the port.

In that same year, a war ship, led by Roberto Bate, attacked the city again, which was bravely defended by the commander of the port and the inhabitants. The Royal Council ordered that no expense be spared in fortifying the city. It was then that the castle El Morro was built with its formidable bastions, and the port of Havana, which was already the most beautiful and the safest in America, also became the most secure. The old Fuerza fortress was almost abandoned; however, taking into consideration its former service and location to the north, they left two garrison soldiers and the original name of Fuerza, adding only the adjective Old.

We will return to this again, my dear daughter. I am already in front of the port, and my emotions are so great that I can barely contain them. Here is the sweet Morro, whose contours appear in the reddish mass of light with its bell and its light marbled dome. Around it float at the wind's mercy and in different directions a thousand flags of different colors that announce the nation and the caliber of the boats that are in the port.

* * *

[The prison of Tacón. Havana. The city's appearance. Santa Clara. Movement and features of the port. The streets and the houses.]

7 in the afternoon

Before me, to the west, El Morro, built next to a rock, rises boldly above the sea... But what has become of the enormous mass that seemed to threaten the sky? Of the colossal rock that in my imagination is as tall as Atlas? Ah! I was mistaken. It doesn't have the same proportions; in place of that heavy and enormous fortress, the tower of El Morro only seems to me daring, delicate, harmonious in its contours, a slender Doric column set on a rock. All human feelings change with time. The castle of El Morro is whitewashed and its shine contrasts with the blackness of the rock and with the gloomy belt formed by the twelve apostles that surround it [twelve heavy-caliber cannons commonly called the twelve apostles].

Now we turn toward the left, the wind behind us; a few fathoms more and we reach the port. Before we enter, above the right shore to the northern side appears a town whose houses, painted in vivid colors, blend in and are confused to the view with the flowering meadows where they appear to have been planted. They seem like a bouquet of wild flowers in the middle of a *parterre*. These are the suburbs of La Luz and of Jesús y María, formerly made up of shacks and now transformed into elegant villas. Like the thought of death on a happy day, a colossal phantasm rises in the middle of these beautiful homes and seems to encircle them with a white canvas... In these thick walls, whose sharp and deadly points can be seen from afar on top of each floor, I recognize the Tacón prison.

A few steps away and surrounded by giant cypresses, a cemetery stands out that didn't exist when I was a child. I recognize this gloomy place by the black cross that, like a dwelling of compassion, extends over the graves. In another time, the ashes of the dead were kept under the flagstones of the church, and in vain one requested a solitary repose below the heavens. Further on, not far from the shore, in the middle of a fiery sandpit at the edge of the sea, is the House of Beneficence.

But behold, my child, that the city begins to merge with the neighbourhoods. Here it is! With its balconies, stores, and flat roofs, with its precious low houses of the middle class, houses with great coach doors, with immense grated windows; the doors and windows are all open here; with a look one can penetrate the intimacies of domestic life, from the flower-covered patio, to the girl's room, whose bed is covered by linen curtains with ties the color of rose. Further on are the aristocratic houses on one floor, surrounded by galleries that announce themselves from a distance by their large rows of green window shades.

I can already pick out the balcony of my father's house, the front of which extends along the front of the Castillo de la Punta. On one side there's a smaller balcony... It was there that, as a child, I contemplated the starry and resplendent sky of the Tropics. There, against the muffled and regular sound of the waves that dissolved in foam on the beach, that my soul exhaled its first perfumes and was lost in religious contemplation. There where, restless, with my eyes fixed on the immensity of the sparkling blue sea, I divined in the frank impulses of my heart that there was a thing as vast as the sea, so unstable, so large, so powerful. I felt this interior world, in which stirred at a distance all human pains and joys, already move away from me, but whose first murmurs reached me accompanied by such pure delights and such delicious harmonies.

Here are the city's bell towers soaring into the sky. Among them I recognize Santa Clara, and I imagine I can distinguish on top the image of Santa Inés, sustained there like a light cloud, with her pale face and her large black eyes! There is the old specter of Dominga the mulatta spying on me through the cloisters with her dim lantern. The illusions and the realities become confused in my troubled brain and make my heart beat as if it wants to leave my chest.

But, what is this I see at the entrance to the city? The terrace of my mother's house! My soul wants to fly toward those places and enter with a sainted respect those walls darkened by time, where the hand of an angel served to support my first steps; where in the shade of her motherly wings, I grew sheltered from the poison shots whose wounds forever tarnish purity. Here was where, always surrounded by examples of goodness and knowledge, I learned to know and love all that is good. Here is where virtue seemed inseparable from our own nature, so naturally and kindly I saw applied its divine precepts to the simplest acts of life... Oh, my daughter, what beautiful inspiration I have obeyed when, in order to fulfill an obligation, I have undertaken such a long and dangerous trip! How many thanks I give to God for having led me through the ocean two thousand miles from my home in order to greet once again the land that witnessed my birth! Teresa, Mariana, my beloved aunts, you who are so young, so beautiful, who fulfilled in such a dignified way your duties to me and the responsibility that the care of a new life imposes, receive the homage of an acknowledging heart. My soul is deeply touched by the sight of these places in which I came into the world among so much love and such tender care and where I have seen blossom such noble inspirations and lovely feelings. Here, charity is practiced in the bosom of the family without ostentation and always accompanied by the enchanting simplicity, the frank candidness of the Creoles, that subdue the heart. Such memories awaken a thousand burning feelings in my heart. Oh, image of my mother, of the dear one of my heart who flies like a gentle mist around this happy dwelling. I greet you. Dear soul, bless me!

But the balconies along our way fill with people, they signal to us, they greet us from all sides. Among the multitude I see many black women in muslin dresses, without stockings or shoes, who carry in their arms babies as white as swans. I also see many young women of slim stature and pale complexion who swiftly walk though the long galleries, with their long black hair loose in floating ringlets, with their diaphanous dresses stirred by the breeze and transparent in the sun... My heart grows heavy, my daughter, to think that I come here as a stranger. The new generation that I am going to meet will not recognize me, and perhaps I will not recognize a large part of the previous generation! Here I am in front of my balcony that extends toward the sea, where all wave, crowd together, reach out their arms, unfold their handkerchiefs, and seem to bet on who will see me first... The house is foreign to me; it doesn't reveal anything of my old memories, and nevertheless, some secret attraction, some mysterious charm, draws me to it. Oh! Yes, it is the house of my Uncle Montalvo, of my friend, my protector, my father; it wasn't necessary for don Salvador, the captain of the slave trader, to tell me; my heart had guessed it.

But, where do those voices mixed with such monotonous and sad cadences come from? As if approaching a torrent, the air fills with wild harmonies, voices that are at once cries and songs. And what songs, God of mercy! If you heard them, my daughter! More than human harmonies, they are like a concert given by the infernal spirits to the king of dusk on a day of ill humor. It is the murmur of the water mixed with the sound of oars moved in all directions by half-naked black men, who row innumerable small boats and shout, smoke, and show us their teeth in a sign of contentment, to welcome us.

We cross wharves populated by a mixed crowd of mulattos and blacks; the first are dressed in white pants and white jackets and covered by large straw hats; the second wear striped linen shorts and colored handkerchiefs tied to their foreheads; the rest wear gray felt hats tipped over the eyes, a red sash fastened carelessly. All sweat in the heat and nevertheless are smart and helpful to us. One sees an infinity of boxes, barrels, bundles on carts, pulled by mules and guided in a negligent manner by a black man in a shirt. In every part there are signs that say coffee, sugar, cocoa, vanilla, camphor, indigo etc. The songs and shouts of those poor Negroes, who don't know how to work except to the beat of noisy shouts marked with pronounced cadences, don't stop for a moment. Everyone moves, everyone is excited, no one stops for a moment. The clearness of the atmosphere adds to this noise, as well as the clearness of the day, something incisive that penetrates the pores and produces a kind of chill. Everything here is life, an animated and burning life like the sun that vibrates its rays on our heads.

We had just dropped the anchor in the middle of a forest of masts and ropes. The passengers prepared their passports; I remembered mine and I could have been looking for it still. After having riffled through all my papers, I find that I have left it in Paris and, nevertheless, I have crossed England and the United States without anyone asking for it. Although it is true that things are done differently here, I trust that I will not have to return without having stepped on my native land. Arriving here is like arriving at my house. What right is more sacred than that of living on the soil where one was born? The only incontestable human possession should be this, the homeland. This first lot that nature has granted us at birth nevertheless isn't more spacious than the last.

A large number of small boats come toward us bearing friends and the curious and customs employees and, among them, a very courteous message from the governor. This is a good sign for the business of my passport. Among the multitude of boats I notice one that hurries and appears in a rush to reach our boat. It is painted white with red trim, and its rowers are dressed in white pants and blue and crimson sashes. They pant, sweat, swell their chests, advance, advance until they touch our *dick*. In it come four young men, the oldest of whom must be twenty years old, who reach out their arms and shake their handkerchiefs. Their clothes are elegant and of good taste, their stature tall, their still adolescent faces are shaded by soft down, and their lively looks bear a pleasant hue of youth and candor. One notices an air of courtesy and delicacy in their persons, and as they show signs of wanting to jump from the boat, one might mistake them for a nest of the most beautiful American birds. They are the sons of my Uncle Montalvo, my cousins. The officers of the Board of Health must come and they haven't come. In the meantime, they treat us as if we were infected, and we are reduced to exchanging a few words with the people who pass in boats around us. Finally, they announce that the representatives of the Faculty of Medicine are eating and, as these gentlemen have the custom of not allowing themselves to be interrupted on such occasions, we are obliged to remain still longer in our dungeon in the fresh air.

I notice a man of advanced age, dressed in black, with the great cross of Isabel the Catholic, with dusty hair, pale face, and fine features, an expressive look and noble bearing; he comes alone standing in a small boat. He calls me, I hear my name, Mercedes; he calls me with a sweet and stirring voice; Mercedes and his eyes, marked by an ineffable expression of kindness, fill up with tears... he calls me and looks at me as if at my mother. Yes, it is he, my dear uncle! I guess it more than I recognize him; I don't find a difference between these two movements of my soul. One might say that at this instant I can see my heart, because I feel my heart, my sight and my memory mix in this living revelation. The boat approaches, followed by other boats. My uncle, my brother, all without doubt come with them. My heart is calling them, I die from anxiety and impatience! Still more boats; finally one of them reaches our ship. It is they... Good-bye, my angel, good-bye.

Translated by Janice Molloy.

TRAVELS THROUGH
THE WEST INDIES

Nancy Gardner Prince

Born on September 15, 1799 in Newburyport, Massachusetts, Nancy Gardner Prince was the granddaughter of Tobias Wornton, a slave who fought in the Battle of Bunker Hill. Her maternal grandmother was Native American. She was the second child of her mother's eight children by the second of her mother's four husbands. Prince's father, Thomas Gardner was born of African descent in Nantucket and died when Prince was three months old.

Prince grew up in Gloucester, Massachusetts. Although she had very little formal education, she "had enjoyed the happy privilege of religious instruction." At the age of twenty-three, she married Mr. Prince and traveled to St. Petersburg, Russia with him. In 1833, Nancy Prince left St. Petersburg for health reasons, while her husband stayed in Russia. Unfortunately he died before he could return.

Upon her return to Boston, Prince attempted to found an orphanage for black children who were denied admittance to other orphanages because of their skin color. She began attending meetings of the anti-slavery societies, and met Reverend Ingraham who sought to enlist help for his mission in Kingston. Seeing a "field of usefulness" spread out before her, Prince volunteered and for the first time, traveled to Jamaica in 1840.

In Jamaica, Prince started her own school for young females who were poor and destitute. She ran the Free Labor School for three months and then returned to Boston in 1843. There, she wrote and published her first book, *A Narrative of the Life and Travels of Mrs. Nancy Prince*, in 1850. By 1856, Prince's health had deteriorated and she had completely lost use of her arms. Circumstances of her life beyond 1856 remain unrevealed.

Prince's narrative includes a travelogue of Copenhagen, St. Petersburg, and the West Indies. She includes details about the Russian culture, the flood of 1824 (where she almost lost her own life), the cholera epidemic of 1831, and more. In her narrative she incorporates a fifteen page pamphlet; *The West Indies: Being a Description of the Islands, Progress of Christianity, Education, and Liberty among the Coloured Population Generally*, detailing the history of slavery and British domination in the West Indies, as well as an account of the Sierra Leone resettlement experiment—all of which is permeated with Prince's repeated denunciation of poverty, inhumanity, and the greed and corruption she observed among the teachers and clergymen of many ethnic backgrounds serving in Jamaica during her visits.

A Black Woman's Odyssey

A denomination under which is comprehended a large chain of islands, extending in a curve from the Florida shore on the northern peninsula of America, to the Gulf of Venezuela on the southern. These islands belong to five European powers, viz: Great Britain, Spain, France, Holland, and Denmark. An inhabitant of New England can form no idea of the climate and the productions of these islands. Many of the particulars that are here mentioned, are peculiar to them all.

The climate in all the West India Islands is nearly all the same, allowing for those accidental differences which the several situations and qualities of the lands themselves produce; as they lie within the tropic of Cancer, and the sun is often almost at the meridian over their heads, they are continually subjected to a heat that would be intolerable but for the trade winds, which are so refreshing as to enable the inhabitants to attend to their various occupations, even under a noonday sun; as the night advances, a breeze begins to be perceived, which blows smartly from the land, as it were from the centre towards the sea, to all points of the compass at once. The rains make the only distinction of seasons on these islands. The trees are green the year round; they have no cold or frost; our heaviest rains are but dews comparatively; with them floods of water are poured from the clouds. About May, the periodical rains from the South may be expected. Then the tropical summer, in all its splendor, makes its appearance. The nights are calm and serene, the moon shines more brightly than in New England, as do the planets and the beautiful galaxy. From the middle of August to the end of September the heat is most oppressive, the sea breeze is interrupted, and calms warn the inhabitants of the periodical rains, which fall in torrents about the first of October.

The most considerable and valuable of the British West India islands, lies between the 75th and the 79th degrees of west longitude from London, and between 17 and 18 north latitude; it is of an oval figure, 150 miles long from east to west, and sixty miles broad in the middle, containing 4,080,000 acres. An elevated ridge, called the Blue Mountains, runs lengthwise from east to west, whence numerous rivers take their rise on both sides. The year is divided into two seasons, wet and dry. The months of July, August, and September, are called the hurricane months. The best houses are generally built low, on account of the hurricanes and earthquakes. However pleasant the sun may rise, in a moment the scene may be changed; a violent storm will suddenly arise, attended with thunder and lightning; the rain falls in torrents, and the seas and rivers rise with terrible destruction. I witnessed this awful scene in June last, at Kingston, the capital of Jamaica; the foundations of many houses were destroyed; the waters, as they rushed from the mountains, brought with them the produce of the earth, large branches of trees, together with their fruit; many persons were drowned, endeavoring to reach their homes; those who succeeded, were often obliged to travel many miles out of their usual way. Many young children, without a parent's care, were at this time destroyed. A poor old woman, speaking of these calamities to me, thus expressed herself: "Not so bad now as in the time of slavery; then God spoke very loud to *Bucker* (the white people) to let us go. Thank God, ever since that they give us up, we go pray, and we have it not so bad like as before." I would recommend this poor woman's remark to the fair sons and daughters of America, the land of the pilgrims. "Then God spoke very loud." May these words be engraved on the post of every door in this land of New England. God speaks very loud, and while his judgments are on the earth, may the inhabitants learn right-eousness!

The mountains that intersect this island, seem composed of rocks, thrown up by frequent earthquakes or volcanoes. These rocks, though having little soil, are adorned with a great variety of beautiful trees, growing from the fissures, which are nour-ished by frequent rains, and flourish in perpetual spring. From these mountains flow a vast number of small rivers of pure water, which sometimes fall in cataracts, from stupendous heights; these, with the brilliant verdure of the trees, form a most delightful landscape. Ridges of small mountains are on each side of this great chain; on these, coffee grows in great abundance; the valleys or plains between these ridges, are level beyond what is usually found in similar situations. The highest land in the island is Blue Mountain peak, 7150 feet above the sea. The most extensive plain is thirty miles long and five broad. Black River, in the Parish of St. Elizabeth, is the only one navigable; flatboats bring down produce from plantations about thirty miles up the river. Along the coast, and on the plains, the weather is very hot; but in the mountains the air is pure and wholesome; the longest days in summer are about thirteen hours, and the shortest in winter about eleven. In the plains are found several salt fountains, and in the mountains, not far from Spanish Town, is a hot bath of great medicinal virtues; this gives relief in the complaint called the drybowels malady, which, excepting the bilious and yellow fevers, is one of the most terrible distempers of Jamaica. The general produce of this island is sugar, rum, molasses, ginger, cotton, indigo, pimiento, cocoa, coffees, several kinds of woods, and medicinal drugs. Fruits are in great plenty, as oranges, lemons, shaddoks, citrons, pomegranates, pineapples, melons, pompions, guavas, and many others. Here are trees whose wood, when dry, is incorruptible; here is found the wild cinnamon tree, the mahogany, the cabbage, the palm, yielding an oil much esteemed for food and medicine. Here, too, is the soap tree, whose berries are useful in washing. The plantain is produced in Jamaica in abundance, and is one of the most agreeable and nutritious vegetables in the world: it grows about four feet in height, and the fruit grows in clusters, which is filled with a luscious sweet pulp. The banana is very similar to the plantain, but not so sweet. The whole island is divided into three counties, Middlesex, Surry, and Cornwall, and these into six towns, twenty parishes, and twenty-seven villages.

This island was originally part of the Spanish Empire in America, but it was taken by the English in 1656. Cromwell had fitted out a squadron under Penn and Venables, to reduce the Spanish island of Hispañola; but there this squadron was unsuccessful, and the commanders, of their own accord, to atone for this misfortune, made a descent on Jamaica, and having arrived at St. Jago, soon compelled the whole island to surrender.

Ever since, it has been subject to the English; and the government, next to that of Ireland, is the richest in the disposal of the crown. Port Royal was formerly the capital of Jamaica; it stood upon the point of a narrow neck of land, which, towards the sea, forms part of the border of a very fine harbor of its own name. The conveniences of this harbor, which was capable of containing a thousand sail of large ships, and of such depth as to allow them to load and unload with the greatest ease, weighed so much with the inhabitants, that they chose to build their capital on this spot, although the place was a hot, dry sand, and produced none of the necessities of life, even fresh water. About the beginning of the year 1692, no place for its size could be compared to this town for trade, wealth, and an entire corruption of manners. In the month of June in this year, an earthquake which shook the whole island to the foundation, totally overwhelmed this city, so as to leave, in one quarter, not even the smallest vestige remaining. In two minutes the earth opened and swallowed up nine-tenths of the houses, and two thousand people. The waters gushed out from the openings of the earth, and the people lay as it were in heaps: some of them had the good fortune to catch hold of beams and rafters of houses, and were afterwards saved by boats. Several ships were cast away in the harbor, and the Swan Frigate, which lay in the dock, was carried over the tops of sinking houses, and did not overset, but afforded a retreat to some hundreds of people, who saved their lives upon her. An officer who was in the town at that time, says the earth opened and shut very quick in some places, and he saw several people sink down to the middle, and others appeared with their heads just above ground, and were choked to death. At Savannah above a thousand acres were sunk, with the houses and people in them, the place appearing, for some time, like a lake; this was afterwards dried up, but no houses were seen. In some parts mountains were split, and at one place a plantation was removed to the distance of a mile. The inhabitants again rebuilt the city, but it was a second time, ten years after, destroyed by a great fire. The extraordinary convenience of the harbor tempted them to build it once more, and in 1722 it was laid in ruins by a hurricane, the most terrible on record.

Such repeated calamities seemed to mark out this spot as a devoted place; the inhabitants, therefore, resolved to forsake it forever, and to reside at the opposite bay, where they built Kingston, which is now the capital of the island. In going up to

Kingston, we pass over a part of and between a Port Royal, leaving the mountains on the left, and a small town on the right. There are many handsome houses built there, one story high, with porticos, and every convenience for those who inhabit them. Not far from Kingston stands Spanish Town, which, though at present far inferior to Kingston, was once the capital of Jamaica, and is still the seat of the government.

The population of Jamaica is nearly 400,000; that of Kingston, the capital, 40,000. There are many places of worship of various denominations, namely, Church of England, and of Scotland, Wesleyan, the Baptist, and Roman Catholics, besides a Jewish Synagogue. These all differ from what I have seen in New England, and from those I have seen elsewhere. The Baptist hold what they call class-meetings. They have men and women deacons and deaconesses in these churches; these hold separate class-meetings; some of these can read, and some cannot. Such are the persons who hold the office of judges, and go round and urge the people to come to the class, and after they come in twice or three times, they are considered candidates for baptism. Some pay fifty cents, and some more, for being baptized; they receive a ticket as a passport into the church, paying one mark a quarter, or more, and some less, but nothing short of ten pence, that is, two English shillings a year. They must attend their class once a week, and pay three pence a week, total twelve English shillings a year, besides the sums they pay once a month at communion, after service in the morning. On those occasions the minister retires, and the deacons examine the people, to ascertain if each one has brought a ticket; if not, they cannot commune; after this the minister returns, and performs the ceremony, then they give their money and depart. The churches are very large, holding from four to six thousand; many bring wood

wood and other presents to their class leader, as a token of their attachment; where there are so many communicants, these presents, and the money exacted, greatly enrich these establishments. Communicants are so ignorant of the ordinance, that they join the church merely to have a decent burial; for if they are not members, none will follow them to the grave, and no prayers will be said over them; these are borne through the streets by four men, the coffin a rough box; not so if they are church members; as soon as the news is spread that one is dying, all the class, with their leader, will assemble at the place, and join in singing hymns; this, they say, is to help the spirit up to glory; this exercise sometimes continues all night, in so loud a strain, that it is seldom that any of the people in the neighbourhood are lost in sleep.

In January, 1823, a society was formed in London for mitigating and gradually abolishing slavery, throughout the British dominions, called the Anti-Slavery Society. His Royal Highness, the Duke of Gloucester, was President of the Society; in the list of Vice Presidents are the names of many of the most distinguished philanthropists of the day, and among them that of the never to be forgotten Mr. Wilberforce; as a bold champion, we see him going forward, pleading the cause of our down-trodden brethren. In the year 1834, it pleased God to break the chains from 800,000 human beings, that had been held in a state of personal slavery; and this great event was effected through the instrumentality of Clarkson, Wilberforce, and other philanthropists of the day.

*   *   *

My mind, after the emancipation in the West Indies, was bent upon going to Jamaica. A field of usefulness seemed spread out before me. While I was thinking about it, the Rev. Mr.

Ingraham, who had spent seven years there, arrived in [Boston]. He lectured in the city at the Marlboro Chapel, on the results arising from the emancipation at the British Islands. He knew much about them, he had a station at a mountain near Kingston, and was very desirous to have persons go there to labor. He wished someone to go with him to his station. He called on me with the Rev. Mr. William Collier, to persuade me to go. I told him it was my intention to go if I could make myself useful, but that I was sensible that I was very limited in education. He told me that the moral condition of the people was very bad, and needed labor aside from any thing else.

*   *   *

Sunday, December 6th, at six o'clock in the evening, dropped anchor at St. Ann harbor, Jamaica. We blessed the Lord for his goodness in sparing us to see the place of our destination; and here I will mention my object in visiting Jamaica. I hoped that I might aid, in some small degree, to raise up and encourage the emancipated inhabitants, and teach the young children to read and work, to fear God, and put their trust in the Savior. Mr. Whitmarsh and his friends came on board and welcomed us. On Tuesday we went on shore to see the place and the people; my intention had been to go directly to Kingston, but the people urged me to stay with them, and I thought it my duty to comply, and wrote to Mr. Ingraham to that effect. I went first to see the minister, Mr. Abbott; I thought as he was out, I had better wait his return. The people promised to pay me for my services, or send me to Kingston. When Mr. Abbott returned he made me an offer, which I readily accepted. As I lodged in the house of one of the class-leaders I attended her class a few times, and when I learned the method, I stopped. She then commenced her authority and gave me to understand if I did not comply I should not have any pay from that society. I spoke to her of the necessity of being born of the spirit of God before we become members of the church of Christ, and told her I was sorry to see the people blinded in such a way.

She was very angry with me and soon accomplished her end by complaining of me to the minister; and I soon found I was to be dismissed, unless I would yield obedience to this class-leader. I told the minister that I did not come there to be guided by a poor foolish woman. He then told me that I had spoken something about the necessity of moral conduct in the church members. I told him I had, and in my opinion, I was sorry to see it so much neglected. He replied, that he hoped I would not express myself so except to him; they have the gospel, he continued, and let them into the church. I do not approve of women's societies; they destroy the world's convention; the American women have too many of them. I talked with him an hour. He paid me for the time I had been there. I continued with the same opinion, that something must be done for the elevation of the children, and it is for that I labor. I am sorry to say the meeting house is more like a play house than a place of worship. The pulpit stands about the middle of the building, behind are the about six hundred children that belong to the society; there they remain until service is over, playing most of the time. The house is crowded with the aged and the young, the greater part of them barefooted. Some have on bonnets, but most of the women wear straw hats such as our countrymen wear.

I gave several Bibles away, not knowing that I was hurting the minister's sale, the people buy them of him at a great advance. I gave up my school at St. Ann, the 18th of March. I took the fever and was obliged to remain until the 7th of April. The people of St. Ann fulfilled their promise which they made to induce me to stop with them. On the 11th of April I arrived at Kingston, and was conducted to the Mico Institution, where Mr. Ingraham directed me to find him; he had lost his pulpit and his school, but Mr. Venning, the teacher, kindly received me. I remained there longer than I expected; the next morning he kindly sent one of the young men with me to the packet for my baggage. I then called on the American Consul, he told me he was very glad to see me for such a purpose as I had in view in visiting Jamaica, but he said it was folly for the Americans to come to the island to better their condition; he said they came to him every day praying him to send them home.

He likewise mentioned to me the great mortality among the emigrants. The same day I saw the Rev. J. S. Beadslee, one of our missionaries, who wished me to accompany him forty miles into the interior of the country.

On May the eighteenth, I attended the Baptist Missionary meeting, in Queen Street Chapel; the house was crowded. Several ministers spoke of the importance of sending the gospel to Africa; they complimented the congregation on their liberality the last year, having given one hundred pounds sterling; they hoped this year they would give five hundred pounds, as there were five thousand members at the present time. There was but one coloured minister on the platform. It is generally the policy of these missionaries to have the sanction of coloured ministers, to all their assessments and taxes. The coloured people give more readily, and are less suspicious of imposition, if one from themselves recommends the measure; this the missionaries understand very well, and know how to take advantage of it. On the twenty-second and twenty-third of June, the coloured

Baptists held their missionary meeting, the number of ministers, coloured and mulattoes, was eighteen, the coloured magistrates were present. The resolutions that were offered were unanimously accepted, and every thing was done in love and harmony. After taking up a contribution, they concluded with song and prayer, and returned home saying jocosely, "they would turn mackroon hunters." "Mack" is the name of a small coin in circulation at Jamaica.

I called, on my return, at the market, and counted the different stalls: for vegetables and poultry, 196 all numbered and under cover, beside seventy on the ground. These are all attended by colored women. The market is conveniently arranged, as they can close the gates and leave all safe. There are nineteen stalls for fresh fish, eighteen for pork, thirty for beef, eighteen for turtle. These are all regular built markets, and are kept by coloured men and women. These are all in one place. Others also may be found, as with us, all over the city. Thus it may be hoped they are not the stupid set of beings they have been called; here *surely we see industry*; they are enterprising and quick in their perceptions, determined to possess themselves, and to possess property besides, and quite able to take care of themselves. They wished to know why I was so inquisitive about them. I told them we had heard in America that you are lazy, and that emancipation has been of no benefit to you; I wish to inform myself of the truth respecting you, and give a true account on my return. Am I right? More than two hundred people were around me listening to what I said.

They thanked me heartily. I gave them some tracts, and told them, if it so pleased God, I would come back to them and bring them some more books, and try what could be done with some of the poor children to make them better. I then left them, and went to the East Market, where there are many of all nations. The Jews and Spanish looked at me very black. The coloured people gathered around me. I gave them little books and tracts, and told them I hoped to see them again.

There are in this street upwards of a thousand young women and children, living in sin of every kind. From thence I went to the jail, where there were seventeen men, but no women. There were in the House of Correction three hundred culprits; they are taken from there, to work on plantations. I went to the Admiral's house, where the emigrants find a shelter until they can find employment, then they work and pay for their passage. Many leave their homes and come to Jamaica under the impression that they are to have their passage free, and on reaching the island are to be found, until they can provide for themselves.

How the mistake originated, I am not able to say, but on arriving here, strangers poor and unacclimated, find the debt for passage money hard and unexpected. It is remarkable that whether fresh from Africa, or from other islands, from the South or from New England, they all feel deceived on this point. I called on many Americans and found them poor and discontented,—rueing the day they left their country, where, notwithstanding many obstacles, their parents lived and died—a country they helped to conquer with their toil and blood; now shall their children stray abroad and starve in foreign lands.

There is in Jamaica an institution, established in 1836, called the Mico Institution. It is named after its founder, Madame Mico, who left a large sum of money to purchase, (or rather to ransom, the one being a Christian act, the other a sin against the Holy Ghost, who expressly forbids such traffic). Madame Mico left this money to ransom the English who were in bondage to the Algerines; if there was any left, it was to be devoted to the instruction of the coloured people in the British isles.

Besides the Mico establishment, there are in Jamaica twenty-seven church missionary schools, where all 952 children are taught gratis. There are sixteen London Missionary Society Schools; the number taught is not ascertained. There are thirty-eight National Schools. There are also the Wesleyan, Presbyterian and Moravian Schools; it is supposed there are private schools, where three or four thousand are educated in the city of Kingston, and twice the number in the street without the means of instruction. All the children and adults taught in the above named schools, are taxed £1 a year, except the English Church School, this is the most liberal. The Rev. Mr. Horton, a Baptist minister in Kingston, told me he had sent ninety children away from the Baptist school because they did not bring their money. It is sufficient to say they had it not to bring!

Most of the people of Jamaica are emancipated slaves, many of them are old, worn out and degraded. Those who are able to work, have yet many obstacles to contend with, and very little to encourage them; every advantage is taken of their ignorance; the same spirit of cruelty is opposed to them that held them for centuries in bondage; even religious teaching is bartered for their hard earnings, while they are allowed but thirty-three cents a day, and are told if they will not work for that they shall not work at all; an extraordinary price is asked of them for every thing they may wish to purchase, even the Bibles are sold to them at a large advance on the first purchase. Where are their apologists, if they are found wanting in the strict morals that Christians ought to practice? Who kindly says, forgive them when they err. "Forgive them, this is the bitter fruit of slavery."

Who has integrity sufficient to hold the balance when these poor people are to be weighed? Yet their present state is blissful, compared with slavery.

Many of the farmers bring their produce twenty or thirty miles. Some have horses or ponys, but most of them bring their burdens on their head. As I returned from St. Andrew's Mountain, where I had been sent for by a Mr. Rose, I was over-taken by a respectable looking man on horseback; we rode about ten miles in company. The story he told me of the wrongs he and his wife had endured while in slavery are too horrible to narrate. My heart sickens when I think of it. He asked me many questions, such as where I came from, why I came to that Isle, where had I lived, &c.. I told him I was sent for by one of the missionaries to help him in his school. Indeed, said he, our colour need the instruction. I asked him why the coloured peo-ple did not hire for themselves? We would be very glad to, he replied, but our money is taken from us so fast we cannot. Sometimes they say we must all bring £1; to raise this, we have to sell at a loss or to borrow, so that we have nothing left for ourselves; the Macroon hunters take all—this is a nickname they give the missionaries and the class-leaders—a cutting sarcasm this!

I arrived at a tavern, about a mile from Kingston, I bade the man adieu, and stopped for my guide. The inn-keeper kindly invited me in; he asked me several questions, and I asked him as many. "How do the people get along," said I, "since the emancipation?" "The negroes," he replied, "will have the island in spite of the d——. Do not you see how they live, and how much they can bear? We cannot do so." This man was an Englishman, with a large family of mulatto children. I returned with my mind fully made up what to do. Spent three weeks at the Mico establishment, and three with my coloured friends from America. We thought something ought to be done for the poor girls that were destitute; they consulted with their friends, called a meeting, and formed a society of forty; each agreed to pay three dollars a year and collect, and provide a house, while I came back to America to raise the money for all needful articles for the school. Here I met Mr. Ingraham for the first time; he had come from the mountains, and his health had rapidly declined. Wishing to get his family home before the Lord took him away, he embarked for Baltimore in the *Orb*, and I sailed for Philadelphia, July 20th, 1841, twenty-one days from Jamaica, in good health.

*   *   *

I collected in Boston and vicinity, in New York and Philadelphia, but not sufficient to make up the required sum, and I was obliged to take fifty dollars from my own purse, thinking that when I returned to Jamaica, they would refund the money to me. April 15th, embarked on board the brig, *Norma*, of New York, for Jamaica. I arrived at Kingston May 6th, and found every thing different from what it was when I left; the people were in a state of agitation, several were hanged, and the insurrection was so great that it was found necessary to increase the army to quell it. Several had been hanged. On the very day I arrived a man was hanged for shooting a man as he passed through the street. Such was the state of things that it was not safe to be there.

A few young people met to celebrate their freedom on an open plain, where they hold their market; their former masters and mistresses, envious of their happiness, conspired against them, and thought to put them down by violence. This only served to increase their numbers; but the oppressors were powerful, and succeeded in accomplishing their revenge, although many of them were relations. There was a rule among the slave holders, to take care of the children they have by their slaves; they select them out and place them in asylums. Those who lived with their white fathers were allowed great power over their slave mothers and her slave children; my heart was often grieved to see their conduct to their poor old grandparents. Those over twenty-one were freed in 1834, all under twenty-one were to serve their masters till twenty-one. It is well known that at that time, the children, alike with others, received twenty-five dollars a head for their relatives. Were I to tell all my eyes have seen among that people, it would not be credited. It is well known that those that were freed, knowing their children were still in bondage, were not satisfied. In the year 1838, general freedom throughout the British Islands gave the death blow to the power of the master, and mothers received with joy their emancipated children; they no longer looked the picture of despair, fearing to see a mulatto son or daughter beating or abusing their younger brothers and sisters of a darker skin. On this occasion there was an outrage committed by those who were in power. What little the poor coloured people had gathered during their four years of freedom, was destroyed by violence; their fences were broken down, and their horses and hogs taken from them. Most of the mulattoes and masters are educated, many of them are very poor, some are very rich; the property is left to the eldest daughter, she divides it with her brothers and sisters; since slavery ended many of them have married; those who are poor, and mean to live in sin, make for New Orleans and other slave States; many of the planters left the island when slavery was abolished. In June, 1841, a number of people arrived from Sierra Leone at Jamaica; these were maroons who were banished from the island. They were some of the original natives who inhabited the mountains, and were determined to destroy the whites. These maroons would secrete themselves in trees, and arrest the whites as they passed along; they would pretend to guide them, when they would beat and abuse them as the whites did their slaves; the English, finding themselves defeated in all their plans to subdue them, proposed to take them by craft. They made a feast in a large tavern in Kingston, and invited them to come. After they had eaten, they were invited on board three ships of war that were all ready to set sail for Sierra Leone; many of them were infants in their mothers' arms, they were well taken care of by the English and instructed; they were removed about the year 1796—they are bright and intelligent; I saw and conversed with them; when they heard of the abolition of slavery, they sent a petition to Queen Victoria that they might return to Jamaica, which was granted. Several of them were very old when they returned; they were men and women when they left the island, they had not forgot the injuries they had received from the hands of man, nor the mercies of God to them, nor His judgments to their enemies. Their numbers were few, but their power was great; they say the island, of right, belongs to them. Had there been a vessel in readiness, I should have come back immediately. It seemed useless to attempt to establish a manual labor School, as the government was so unsettled that I could not be protected. Some of my former friends were gone as teachers to Africa, and some to other parts of the island. I called on the American Consul to consult with him; he said that although such a school was much wanted, yet every thing seemed so unsettled that I had no courage to proceed. I told him there was so much excitement that I wished to leave the island as soon as he could find me a passage, it seemed useless to spend my time there. As soon as it was known that I intended to return, a movement was made to try to induce me to remain. I was persuaded to try the experiment for three months, not thinking their motive was bad. Before I left the United States, I got all that was needed, within fifty dollars. The fifty dollars I got from my own purse, expecting they would pay me. It cost me ten dollars for freight, and twenty-five for passage money; these people that I had hoped to serve were much taken up with the things I had brought, they thought that I had money, and I was continually surrounded; the thought of colour was no where exhibited, much notice was taken of me. I was invited to breakfast in one place, and to dine in another, &c. A society was organized, made up of men and women of authority. A constitution was drafted by my consent, by those who were appointed to meet at my rooms. Between the time of the adjournment they altered it to suit themselves. At the time appointed we came together with a spirit apparently becoming any body of Christians; most of them were members of Christian churches. The meeting was opened with reading the Scriptures and prayer. Then said the leader, since our dear sister has left her native land and her friends to come to us, we welcome her with our hearts and hands. She will dwell among us, and we will take care of her— Brethren think of it!—after which he sat down, and the constitution was called for. The Preamble held out all the flattery that a fool could desire; after which they commenced the articles, supposing that they could do as they thought best. The fourth article unveiled their design. As we have designed to take care of our sister, *we the undersigned will take charge of all she has brought*; the vote was called, every person rose in a moment except myself: every eye was upon me; one asked me why I did not vote, I made no answer—they put the vote again and again, I remained seated. Well, said the president, we can do nothing without her vote; they remained some time silent, and then broke up the meeting. The next day the deacon called to see what the state of my mind was, and some of the women proposed that we should have another meeting. I told them no, I should do no more for them. As soon as they found they could not get the things in the way they intended, they started to plunder me; but I detected their design, and was on my guard. I disposed of the articles, and made ready to leave when an opportunity presented. A more skillful plan than this, Satan never designed, but the power of God was above it. It is not surprising that this people are full of deceit and lies, this is the fruits of slavery, it makes master and slaves knaves. It is the rule where slavery exists to swell the churches with numbers, and hold out such doctrines as *obedience to tyrants* as duty to God. I went with a Baptist woman to the house of a minister to have her grandchild christened before it died; she told me if she did not have it christened, it would rise up in judgment against her. This poor deluded creature was a class-leader in the Baptist Church, and such is the condition of most of the people: they seemed blinded to every thing but money. They are great for trade, and are united in their determination for procuring property, of which they have amassed a vast amount. Notwithstanding I had made over various articles to one of the American missionaries, a Mr. J.S.O. Beadslee, of Clarendon Mountains, I also gave to others, where they were needed, which receipts and letters I have in my possession. Notwithstanding all this, they made another attempt to rob me, and as a passage could not be obtained for me to return home, I was obliged to go to the Mico establishment again for safety, such was the outrage. Houses were broken open and robbed every night. I came very near to being shot: there was a certain place where we placed ourselves the first of the evening. A friend came to bring us some refreshments, I had just left the window when a gun was fired through it, by one that often sat with us; this was common in the time of slavery. Previous to vessels arriving, passages were engaged. I disposed of my articles and furniture at a very small profit. On the 1st of August, Capt. A. Miner arrived, and advertised for passengers. The American Consul procured me a passage, and on the 18th of August, myself and nine other passengers embarked for New York.

TRAVELS THROUGH CHILE

Ana du Rousier and the Sacred Heart Nuns

INTRODUCTION

Ana du Rousier, who founded the Society of the Sacred
Heart in Chile in 1853, was born in France, in the Poitou
region, cradle of Vendean resistance to the French Revolution,
in 1806.

When she was eight years old, an event took place which permanently affected her life and her personality. She was standing
in the doorway of the family castle of Lambertiere, when the
Baron du Rousier, her father, was brought home battered and
killed, carried home in a hand barrow by some peasants.
Presumably, it was a political murder.

From then on, Ana decided never again to give her heart to
anyone who could be torn away from her thus. From then on,
sadness and a certain rigidity mark ber character, which was
also affected by the French Jansenism of that time.

As a young novice she was sent to Italy, to the Piedmont. In Turin she worked in the school for nobles founded by the Congregation in 1823, under the patronage of King Carlos Félix and his wife María Cristina. Next to the school there was also—as was the custom in all the Congregation's schools—a free elementary school for poor children.

The revolutionary movements in Italy caused her expulsion from Turin and the closing of the school in 1848. Saint Magdalena Sofia, founder of the Society of the Sacred Cross, sent her next to the United States to visit the Houses established years before by the first missionary of the Congregation: Saint Rosa Filipina Duchesne. Ana du Rousier arrived in Saint Louis, Louisiana in November 1852, shortly before the death of Rosa Filipina, as though to receive the torch from her which she would carry to Chile and from there to all of South America.

That same year, accompanied by Monsignor Joaquín Larraín Gandarillas—future founder of the Catholic University of Chile—and by two other nuns, Mary MacNally, an Irishwoman, and Antonieta Pissorno, an Italian, she set forth on her difficult and long journey to Chile.

Her passage across the isthmus of Panama almost cost her her life and reveals clearly the iron will and determination of this missionary whose generosity, intelligence and extraordinary love overcame all obstacles.

They reached Chile on September 12, 1853, and in Santiago they founded the first Normal School for Chilean women, at the request of President Manuel Montt.

It was inaugurated on the Plazoleta de San Isidro on February 2, 1854 and in 1860, it moved to the building constructed on Portugal Street, called La Maestranza

In 1858, she founded the Colegio de Talca, which was later

destroyed twice by earthquakes. In 1865, she founded the Colegio de Concepción, also destroyed by an earthquake, but the reconstructed building is still there today. In 1869 she founded the Valparaíso House which later was moved to Viffa del Mar and today is located in Reffaca. In 1873, the Chilean government entrusted her with the Normal School for teachers in Chillán.

In 1876 she sent a group of nuns to Lima, Perú to found the first Normal School in Peru in order to train teachers. The School is still functioning in Montemco. And a few months before she died, she organized the foundation of a House in Buenos Aires, Argentina, by a group of nuns who would go around Cape Horn by ship to get there.

Ana du Rousier died in La Maestranza on January 29, 1880, a "Chilean in her heart." She left a permanent mark on Chile through her educational mission, which affected women of all social classes, and especially through the training of thousands of teachers who then carried the values learned from her and her companions out to schools scattered in the most remote corners of Chile.

—Paz Riesco
Convent of the Sacred Heart
Santiago, Chile

I. TRAVEL JOURNAL OF MOTHER DU ROUSIER, MME. TALON, MME. LESIRE AND SISTERS RICHARD AND ANTONIETTA, FROM PARIS TO CHILE. MAY 9, 1852 (WRITTEN BY MME. LESIRE)

My Reverend Mother (Santa Magdalena Sofia):
How it fills me with joy that my worthy Mother [Ana du

Rousier] should have chosen me to be her humble secretary! It provides me with a welcome opportunity of which I have been deprived for all too long: that of expressing my gratitude and offering my tender and respectful appreciation. I rejoice in the momentary illusion which allows me to forget the distance that separates us, and I feel very close to you, my Reverend Mother, as I here provide you with an account of the details of our journey. It makes me smile to imagine you reacting in some alarm. Yes, I am imagining all that, because my heart and thoughts are with you in Paris and I feel myself close to my Venerated Mothers; I hear your good counsel and your wise warnings; I am filled with eagerness, and I am inspired to follow your words and even more your saintly examples.

As I already said, my Reverend Mother, our Mother conferred upon me the welcome task of recounting the story of our journey. I will begin the account with our departure from Le Havre.

May 9, Sunday, around 10:30 in the morning. We stepped aboard the *Neustrie*, a small steamship which would deliver us to our ocean-going ship, anchored some distance from shore. It was a truly solemn moment, my Reverend Mother, when the last mooring ropes were cast off and the heavy gangplank was pulled aboard! At that moment, we were totally cut off from France! The boat began to pull out, and everyone crowded to the rail as if to bid our beloved France a final farewell. A profound silence followed the clamor of all the good-byes being called back and forth. I think we nuns renewed our vows to the Lord, from the bottoms of our hearts, and pledged to sacrifice ourselves for His greater glory and the salvation of souls. And, oh, how aware we were at that moment of the grace conferred by our Venerated Mothers' blessings and the prayers of our beloved sisters!

A half hour later, we went aboard the *Humboldt*, a fine commercial ship, 290 feet long. It flew a flag with two olive branches on it, a symbol of peace, a message which we felt in our hearts despite the bitterness of our sacrifice. We sat on the deck while our Sisters Richard and Antonietta went off to get the numbers of our cabins. Unfortunately, since we had not chosen them ahead of time, we were given the last ones, that is, the darkest and smallest ones where the motion of the boat is most felt. Our Worthy Mother and Mrs. Talon occupied the first one; Julia and I were in the second one. We were just across from a gentleman who was always sick due to his pronounced taste for liquor, especially for brandy. A little farther aft, Julia found an unoccupied cabin across from Our Mother's, and she installed herself there in order to provide us with nursing care, since she was only seasick for two days. Her help was truly Providential for the rest of us.

Monday, May 10. We were at anchor all morning across from the Isle of Wight, and several passengers from there boarded the ship. During the day, the sea became rougher and our great trials began that afternoon. Our Mother had supplied us with an enchanting and short set of rules which provided ample time for our religious exercises during our moments of leisure. But, oh, we had to content ourselves with simply contemplating these written guidelines and with offering Our Lord our good intentions during the day. Our Mother had retired to the second class section, where our Sisters shared a four-bed cabin with a half crazy young woman who amused the passengers during the crossing with her ridiculous antics. Since the rocking of the ship was felt less in that cabin, Our Mother had chosen it as our little oratory. But she soon felt so ill that, had it not been for Julia, she would have remained there. Not one of us was able to stand on her feet. We remained thus until Thursday when the kindly Captain, who visited us every day, obliged us so firmly to get up, that we managed to get to the sitting room, still dressed in our sleeping caps and night shirts. There we stretched out on the benches in the company of several other ladies who were as sick as we were.

It was there that we got better acquainted with a French lady and her uncle, and with Mrs. Kerney, who was a good friend of Mrs. Causans. Meanwhile, the sea got rougher and rougher. Many passengers who were making the crossing for the 15th, 20th or even the 30th time, agreed that they had never experienced such heavy waves. Sister Antonietta felt sure that her last hour had come and picking up a small statue of the Holy Virgin, she put it at the porthole of her cabin exclaiming: "This is the end; we are sinking! Holy Virgin, bless the sea!" Then she repeated the Act of Contrition 22 times, believing each time that it was the end of her life.

Saturday, May 15. This was one of the worst days. The boat rocked so, that one gentleman fell from the top of a stairway and broke his kneecap. Many people fell down during lunch and in the afternoon, the tea suddenly spilled onto the floor, together with the tea cakes and the broken cups. The sounds of smashing dishes, bottles and glasses could be heard everywhere. It was nine at night and no one wanted to retire, despite the exhausting events of the day. Somehow we were all afraid to separate, when an even louder crash made us fear a new accident. In effect: an enormous panel had just knocked over five sailors who were busy hoisting a sail and one of them broke his arm. Our Mother seemed to forget her own illness in order to tend to us. She went from one sitting room to another to bring us news and she tried to calm down a poor wetnurse who, beyond herself with fear, was invoking all the saints in Paradise, crying out for her husband and children whom she had left in Paris, and then she yelling at the children with more than energetic expressions.

Around 10:30, we sought our cabins, not without some contusions, and we spent the rest of the night going back and forth in distress, constantly running the risk of slipping in the passageways.

After Sunday, we were no longer quite so ill; that is, we vomited less continuously. We left our cabins as soon as we could, since the motion was unbearable in them and we got together with our two friends and the Sisters of Charity in the little Gentlemen's Sitting Room, where both men and ladies spent the better part of the day gambling large sums of money. Several of them lost as much as 1500 francs during the course of one afternoon.

Joining our group of close acquaintances was a nice Protestant gentleman, whose wife we had helped to care for. From then on, he became our protector and managed to obtain excellent service for us when we arrived at Customs, as well as taking upon himself the responsibility of conveying us to Harlem himself, after having had our luggage taken to our coach.

May 18. We began to be in real danger, according to our captain, who spent three days and three nights keeping watch on deck, stopping the ship every little while to take soundings and to try to locate the ice floes that were smashing against the boat. They could have damaged it, since were we we were on the shoals of the Bank of Newfoundland, in such a dense fog that it was not possible to see from one side of the ship to the other.

Wednesday 19. God sent us a somewhat calmer night and we all tried to take advantage of it, going to bed earlier than usual. Fear had brought Sister Antonietta to my cabin, where she took Julia's place, giving herself over to her sad thoughts in solitude. For her, the sailors' songs were a bad augury and made her anxious. The Captain's whistle, which was blown every quarter of an hour to announce our presence to smaller vessels, made her think of robbers. And thus, she got into her bunk reluctantly, asking me "So you are really going to sleep now?" "Yes, Sister, if I can!..." "Ah well, then I will keep listening, because they say there is danger and I do not want to die without warning. Good night." She listened so well that around midnight, when she heard a little more noise, she got up quietly and went to Mother du Rousier's cabin. "My Mother, My Mother, are you asleep?" Our Mother woke up with a jump. "Yes, Sister, what do you want?" "Oh I am so afraid!" "Why, since all is so calm?" "What do you mean? Haven't you heard that we've come to the end of our days? We are going to drown!" "No, go back to bed and sleep." "Yes, Mother." Sister Antonietta went off and then returned, choked with emotion, to say to Our Mother: "If you would bless me, then I will be able to die in peace." Our Mother blessed her and she came and lay down again somewhat calmed, since she saw me sleeping so profoundly that I had not even heard her get up. Afterward, she told me that at that moment she had made an Act of Contrition in my name.

Suddenly, the noise increased and the poor Sister, unable to bear any more, called to me "Eh, you're sleeping. Don't you hear? Now we are surely going to die! My Lord Jesus!" "But Sister, calm down, all that's happening is that they are raising the sails. There is no danger. On the contrary, it is a good sign. The wind is favorable for us and we will sail along twice as fast."

"Ah, so it is all right then?" "Yes, let's sleep." "Oh, I don't think I can. I will say my Act of Contrition." Just at that moment, some steam was released and the poor Sister's alarm was intensified more than ever. "My Lord Jesus! What are they doing now with the pots and pans? What a cook we have; he is going to blow us all up!" I laughed so hard that I was totally unable to calm her. Her only consolation was in repeating: "I have Our Mother's blessing, so now the fish can eat me if I drown. Of course I would rather have died in my bed."

I do not need to tell you, my Reverend Mother, how we united ourselves in heart and desire with your whole privileged family on the Day of the Ascension! Oh, how sad and gloomy that day was for us. Our happiness lay in thinking of yours and that of our dear students. If I did not fear boring you with my many words, I would tell you a bit more about our doctor. He has a pronounced liking for the French language, but unfortunately his own ability to express himself never quite matches up with his desires. Thus, our Mother du Rousier's solemn look was all that kept us from laughing when we heard him tell his little anecdotes, which I will pass on to my students. I will only transmit literally to you, my Reverend Mother, the following exchange: "Mre. etre malade?" "Yes, doctor. I can't bear this any more. My illness so is violent that I vomited blood this morning." "*Oui, aie, aie, la mer etre assez haute, oui, oui, demain desperance que l'oné etre plus, aie, aie, etre plus baissée, plus calme, oui, j'ai l'honneur de salouer son Madame.*" Many of his utterances were addressed to me, so I can assure you that this is an authentic transcription. Let us say that on board the ship the doctor demonstrated his graciousness but that was all...

Sunday, May 23. Finally, during a beautiful sunset, we greeted America with a ten-gun salute, which was answered immediately from New York. Our worthy Mother would have liked to take us to Harlem right away, but despite her efforts, we had to spend the night on board, where our neighbor across the way made us spend a very bad night. This poor man had so enjoyed the Captain's champagne, that he was unable to stand up and he fell into the sea when he tried to disembark in the afternoon. Miraculously, they rescued him and closed him up in his cabin where he made a huge commotion throughout the entire night. Sister Antonietta cried out in agony from her side: "Lord, have mercy on that wastrel who is making it impossible for Our Mother to sleep and us, too."

Finally, after many tribulations and thanks to Mr. Lemercier's help, we arrived in Harlem at one o'clock, after lunch. Imagine their surprise and amazement! No one was expecting us, but tender charity never lacks in the Sacred Heart, and we were greeted as warmly by our Mothers of America as we would have been in France. However, we dare to say that neither this generous reception nor their kindnesses could ever make us forget about our Venerated Mothers and beloved Sisters. We reiterate to you our efforts to be your humble and grateful daughters in the Hearts of Jesus and of Mary.

(Account written by Anais Lesire, RSCJ,
born in France in 1827)

CROSSING THE ISTHMUS OF PANAMA IN 1853
A CHAPTER FROM THE LIFE OF ANA DU ROUSIER

For an account of crossing the isthmus of Panama, a strange trip which seems part of a remote age, since civilization in other regions has progressed so much, let us listen to the words of a trustworthy eyewitness:

The railroad journey, quite short then, revealed such abundant and surprising vegetation that, in awe of those marvels of nature, we praised the Lord a thousand times over. Our enthusiasm did not last long; less than an hour had gone by when we had to step down under a blazing sun because the train did not go any farther. They had worried a lot about how to arrange Reverend Mother du Rousier's journey; an American lady assured them from her own experience that a litter or hammock was the only resort for a person who could not ride a horse, but good porters would be needed for this, and they were not easy to find then, and they would demand four hundred pesetas. Although the expense was nothing for those gentlemen, who were confident that they were conveying a treasure to their country, they were afraid of sunstroke, a great danger under that blazing sun for someone in the position required by a hammock. They decided finally that Mother du Rousier would take a mule.

When we got to Barbacoa, we followed the other travelers to a house which serves as an inn, where we found ourselves paying for food which the Mexicans devoured right under our eyes, something that happened every time we joined the others, because food was very scarce and some travelers were unscrupulous about satisfying their stomachs at another's cost. Having enjoyed the disquieting spectacle of seeing others eat, we went to the pier, where we found a new kind of transport to take us to the city of Cruz. Over a hundred canoes were waiting at the edge of the river to take travelers and baggage. These canoes are made from tree trunks; six black men, almost naked, with long poles in their hands, that they poke into the mud, hurry the embarkation along, yelling horribly throughout the whole operation. With the help of some boards and ropes, and sustained

by our guides, we finally reached the boat and while the gentlemen were conversing with each other, we said our prayers in a
kind of pavilion erected on the fore deck. The crossing took
seven hours; sometimes the canoe could not move forward
because the water was too shallow and then the black men
exerted themselves so, that sweat ran abundantly down their
evil looking faces animated by liquor; Sister Antonia was indig-
nant about their savage yells and the skimpiness of their garments. Otherwise the jungle during the daytime was really
enchanting: birds of all kinds and with gorgeous plumage
seemed to ask us why we were interrupting their peace. At night,
the spectacle changed; the jungle looked dark and ominous to
us; only by thinking that the angels were watching at our sides
could we dispel our fear, since night is the time when the wild
beasts that have their dens there awake.

We reached Cruz ahead of the other travelers, thanks to a
good tip we gave our rowers, and thus we managed to find a
room in which to spend the night; it was about five meters
square, and held three wretched beds and a table, and had a
window without glass panes. Our companions were put into the
room next door. At dinnertime, we went down to a great hall
where we saw, by the light of a few candles, many men with
unwholesome faces that made us tremble. Following the advice
we had been given, we tried to hide our fears under a serene and
tranquil look in order not to irritate those frightening men by
showing our mistrust and apprehension. With great difficulty,
the Peruvian businessman managed to open passage for us
between those bandits, who barely moved in order to let us
squeeze through, looking at us from foot to toe as though sizing
us up. Finally, overcoming a thousand difficulties, we managed
to sit down at the table, occupied already by all those who had

paid; the rest were on foot and, forming a tightly packed mass, grabbed all the dishes that the waiters were bringing to us, and if by chance, one made its way to us, it disappeared instantly due to the skill of the bandits who were leaning over the backs of our chairs. Thanks to the firm and determined attitude of our companions, we finally succeeded in eating a beef steak and a piece of bread that had barely felt the heat of the oven and of which flour seemed the least plentiful ingredient. Without hope of eating anything else, we left that battlefield and went back to our tiny room. There close by were the Canon Mr. Herrera and Mr. Larraín, reciting the words of the breviary, and to calm us they said they would keep watch through the night, guarding us from their adjoining room, separated from ours only by a partition; thus, if we made the slightest sound, they would come to see what was going on, reminding us to bolt the door, because the house was full of thieves. The next morning we were awakened by Sister Antonia exclaiming loudly, "Come quickly and see the plaza, it is all full of camels." The camels were the mules prepared for the travelers, some loaded up with baggage, others saddled for riders, etc. so the whole group presented a very curious spectacle. Before mounting our steeds, we had to get dressed in the appropriate clothes for the circumstances and the excessive heat: some black and white skirts of a very lightweight cloth substituted for the usual riding costume, raincoats to protect us from the rain, and some round hats that we had bought the day before in Aspinwall. We were finishing preparing when Mr. Larraín came to tell us we could hear Mass in a place that still bears the name of church. It was a building in ruins, even sadder and more lugubrious inside than out; the walls were black and dirty, the floor made with remains of tombstones, and the altar of stone, held up by two broken columns and covered by a scrap of rag. The corners were full of old trunks, boxes and barrels, and everything was so dirty that it was obvious that no one had ever been in there with a broom. In a niche there was a doll four or five feet tall that was supposed to represent the Holy Virgin, dressed in an old black dress and with a cotton headdress. When upon entering we saw Canon Mr. Herrera kneeling before the altar, we understood that he was making amends to His Divine Majesty for being thus unworthily housed. After Mass we tried to have breakfast, but the scenes of the night before took place again, with worse results, because the second we had a cup of coffee in front of us, someone would snatch it away so fast we couldn't even smell its aroma. Convinced of the futility of our efforts, we got up from the table, after having paid for a breakfast we never got to taste.

It was seven in the morning when we mounted our steeds; Sister Antonia led the march, accompanied by Mr. Herrera and Don Manuel. Mr. Larraín stayed with Mother du Rousier and did not leave her for a single instant during such a dangerous journey, constantly lending her his services since the black men he had hired to lead the mule did their job very badly. For half an hour we walked along a rocky trail, full of ruts from the continuous rains, and then we had to forge our way along narrow, steep trails that flood torrents and streams had formed between the rocks, and so that our feet would not be bashed by the rocks, we had to sit Carmelite style on top of the saddle, sometimes leaning down over the mule's head when it was scrambling up a steep slope, or leaning backwards when it was descending a precipice. Any other exercise of equitation was useless, there was nothing to do but let the mule follow its instinct and sit firmly in the saddle, trying not to be frightened by the shakes, jumps and whimsies of that indomitable animal.

Sometimes it would stop as though to calculate the distance and then suddenly it would leap and cover a six or seven foot gap; each one of these jumps reminded us of the story of the Sister of Charity hurled to the bottom of a precipice. The Reverend Mother du Rosier, as a precaution, was going along very slowly, so soon the first part of the caravan, led by Sister Antonia, got way ahead of us. We stayed with Mr. Larraín, his brother Don Ladislao, Colonel Izarnótegui, an attache of the Peruvian Legation, another gentleman from that country and a black servant of Mr. Herrera's, who had left him to take care of Mother du Rousier's mule.

A circumstance that greatly increases the dangers of the isthmus crossing is that of meeting caravans coming the opposite direction; the steamships that come from the Gulf of Mexico arrive at the same time as those from the Pacific, and the travelers cross halfway along the trail. If they meet on open ground there is nothing to fear; but if they are in a narrow canyon, you have to go back as quickly as possible in order not to be squashed against the rocks by the mules and the baggage. To avoid the danger, the mule drivers, when they enter a very narrow stretch, begin to call out at the top of their lungs, to give warning of their presence and avoid an encounter. We were also about to see ourselves in that situation and to once again recognize the generous intervention of Divine Providence. We were quite a way into a torturous canyon, so narrow and steep that we could only see a blue line of sky above our heads. Rocks surrounded us on all sides when, as we got to a curve in the trail, we heard the shout of a mule driver warning that a caravan was thundering down upon us. Don Ladislao turned around to us terrified, crying out "What shall we do?" But before anyone could answer him, the first mule appeared, loaded with enormous bundles and right behind him another twenty that charged down onto us as rapidly as their heavy burdens allowed. Our guides ran out with their arms open to stop them, but it was all in vain. Without time to deliberate, each one jumped to the ground however he could, some climbing trees, and others clambering up rocks until the caravan had gone past. It was not possible to get the Reverend Mother down from her mule so quickly and she fell, hit by a loaded mule. Fortunately, she fell into a hole full of dirt so the blow was somewhat softened; some pointed rocks protected her and above all the Heart of Jesus, because it was a true miracle that she was not smashed to death. After the caravan had gone by, giving a thousand thanks to the Lord for having escaped from the danger with only a few scratches, the Reverend Mother du Rousier got back up on her mule, which had a smashed stirrup, girth and bridle, and so that nothing should be missing, during this whole incident our guides and the other mule drivers had been vomiting insults and blasphemies continuously.

In the isthmus of Panama the blacks consider themselves to be the owners and lords, since only they are familiar with those labyrinths of torturous trails, and it seems that there they avenge themselves for the slavery that whites make them suffer in other places. One from the other caravan, taking advantage of this arbitrary principle, stopped Sister Antonia's mule, vowing that she could go no farther. The Marquis of la Pica, who had taken her under his protection, commanded the black man to leave her way open, and since he still resisted, swearing a thousand insults, he threatened him with his loaded pistol. The black man had to cede, but to avenge himself, he shoved the poor Sister so hard that she tumbled onto the ground. We did not find out about this incident until later.

No sooner had we escaped from one danger than we were threatened by another: around noon the sun suddenly clouded over and we began to hear thunder announcing an imminent rainstorm. We had heard so much about how grandiose a spectacle a storm could be in that country, that we were not displeased to see it come, as long as it should respect our persons; out of prudence we immediately put on our raincoats and our straw hats. Just as soon as we had taken these precautions, the cataracts of the sky opened, a true flood began and the trails became unusable. Before us we had an extensive jungle, whose leafy giant trees offered a lugubrious sight: to take shelter there seemed foolhardy, and to leave us in peril of being threatened by a lightning bolt any instant; but without even commenting on this, we entrusted ourselves to God and followed the guides. As we moved on ahead, the trail became more and more difficult. The mules were sinking into the mud. They could not forge ahead and we were soaked through to the bone and were covered with mud up to our waists. Finally, little by little, the lightning became less frequent and we reached a little hut, where we stopped to give the mules some water. The blacks wanted to have some refreshment, too, but they drank too much of that perfidious liquor and we suffered the consequences because they stopped paying attention to the mules. At that point we were following a very narrow track, with a precipice on one side and a swampy lake on the other. Since we had been told to let the mules follow their instinct about the trail, we did not guide them and almost all of them sank into the mud. Suddenly Colonel Izarnótegui let out a cry that appalled us; we turned around to look behind us and, oh my God!, the Reverend Mother du Rousier had disappeared. Mr. Larraín raised his eyes and his hands to the sky as though pleading for help. The mule had fallen at the end of the precipice and the mule drivers were looking into the abyss yelling "The lady has fallen!" What a terrible moment! Only God knows how we suffered, but His Divine Providence always watches over his Brides. The mule, stumbling, had hurled our Reverend Mother into the abyss and, without God's aid, she would have smashed against the rocks as she tumbled down more than a hundred feet. The Mother says that in the moment of falling, she placed herself totally in the hands of Our Lord and, as though an angel had providentially put it there, she rolled into a tree trunk she could hold onto, hanging over the edge of the abyss. Mr. Larraín immediately ordered the blacks to climb down and rescue her. But promises, threats, everything was useless, and the Mother was too drained of energy to let go of the tree trunk and crawl up the slope herself, when Manuel, Mr. Herrera's black servant, furious at such resistance, caught another black man by the shoulders and obliged him to go down with him, risking his life, because the danger was imminent and there was no place to brace a foot, but then, no doubt about it, God sent His angels to help him and blessed his generous action. He got down to the place where our Mother was lying nearly unconscious by now, but resigned to everything. By obliging the mule drivers to help him, handing down ropes to him, he managed to climb up with his precious cargo to the edge of the steep precipice. It is easy to imagine what state Mother du Rousier must have been in, covered with scrapes and contusions, although, thanks be to God, without any serious injuries. Mr. Larraín couldn't stop giving thanks to the Almighty for such a miraculous rescue and repeated over and over again: "How God loves them! How God loves them!" Helped by the black servant who had saved her life, Mother du Rousier managed to get back up on the mule with great effort and Colonel Izarnótegui stayed right by her side from now on. But their misfortunes had not yet come to an end: that mule seemed to be an instrument of the Devil to impede the foundation of the Order in Chile. Instead of walking around a deep pool of mud on the path, as the other mules had, her mule walked straight into it, sinking in up to his ears. The poor Mother was entirely covered with mud; she truly seemed on this trip to be a victim destined for martyrdom, and her companions themselves say that it is a miracle that she survived that journey. Colonel Izarnótegui wringing his hands exclaimed: "She will die, she will die, it is impossible that this Lady can endure more;" and in effect she could no longer stand up, nor even lift up her dress. Soaked as it was in gluey mud, her skirt had to be cut off her. After this incident Mr. Larraín switched mules with her, until they could find a hammock.

We moved forward so slowly that it seemed impossible that we would reach Panama before nightfall, although our companions wished this at all costs, because it was not at all appealing to them to spend a night in a forest inhabited by blacks, thieves and slaves, all of them greedy for travelers' money.

At four o'clock we came to a kind of inn, quite clean, which had the following sign on it: "Lodging here for people on foot and on horseback." A Frenchman who was there encouraged us strongly to stay there, saying that it was foolhardy to continue the journey and that the caravan that had gone on ahead would already have reached the point where we were going to meet.

Our Reverend Mother, who could barely continue the journey, would have been happy to follow this advice, which seemed very prudent, because night was not far off, but out of courtesy she acceded to the desire of the gentlemen who wanted to meet up with Canon Herrera and the Peruvian businessman. We had about four more miles to go, or two hours of travel, to get to the meeting place agreed upon, although it was not probable that they would still be waiting for us. We started off and two hours later, we reached the famous hut. When we asked about the earlier caravan, with three blacks who looked ferocious, which was headed for the port, they answered that it had passed by there at three o'clock without stopping and that at nine that night they would get to Panama; that meant that we still had six more hours on the road to go, even if everything went smoothly. It was impossible for Mother du Rousier to continue the journey in the pitiful state she was in. The blacks could see that we were dead with fatigue but they did not offer us the hut. Mr. Larraín asked them for something to eat, and they answered that they did not have anything. Just then, a girl arrived bringing some milk. We accepted it in order not to die of hunger, although it was completely sour. Finally we decided to get down off our mules, after thirteen hours of continuous travel. The Reverend Mother du Rousier rested for a few moments in a broken down chair, and Mr. Larraín began negotiations with the blacks for them to rent us a hammock that they had hanging up in the doorway. At first they did not pay any attention to him, and would not even answer his questions. After a while, one of them named Encarnación said insolently that there was no hammock around there, and when he pointed to it with his finger, she answered, laughing at our desperate situation, that she would not give it to him. We offered her five duros, ten, fifteen, but far from accepting, she answered with a rain of insults about whites and in particular about priests and monks. Mother MacNally wanted to know what Encarnación was saying. "Be thankful to God that you do not understand her," Mr. Larraín replied. Seeing that we had resolved to continue the journey, without accepting the black's belated offer to let us spend the night in his hut, God knows with what intentions, he went off to consult his companions and a little later he came back and said they would be willing to carry the hammock and come with us. While the other two blacks made their preparations, Encarnación sharpened a two-edged knife right in front of us, and loaded the shotgun, saying betgween her teeth: "The one who gets shot with this isn't going to be walking around any more!" Getting more and more uneasy, and with very dark forebodings, since our fears seemed all too reasonable, we helped Mother du Rousier to get into the miserable hammock, its ends slung over the shoulders of the two black men. The rest of us mounted our mules and in complete silence, as though it were a funeral procession, we followed our guides through the total darkness. The gentlemen rode alongside the hammock, except for Don Ladislao, who went on ahead to explore the terrain, saying that the sound of him falling would alert the rest of us to danger. As she left the cabin, Mother MacNally told him that she was reassured now that they had found a comfortable way to transport Mother du Rousier. "Well, I am not," he replied, "because we are carrying a shipment of gold and my brother is unarmed; I have two pistols and my dagger, but they will be of little use against all the blacks of the country if they arc conniving with the guides, as Manuel suspects. Pray a lot because I only trust in God." Every few minutes Don Ladislao called to his brother to make sure that nothing had happened to him, and we all moved ahead, staying very alert, fearful of the slightest noise, when suddenly we heard in a distance the hoof beats of many mules coming closer and closer. When we had them in sight, we took a deep breath: they were the Mexicans who had come with us on the *Georgia*, and although their company might not be very agreeable, they would be able to defend us in case of necessity, so Don Ladislao begged them to pause for a few moments so that our caravan might join theirs. But without paying any attention to our pleas, they speeded up their pace and soon were lost to sight.

We had been traveling for an hour through the dusk when we reached a cabin of sorts, where there was light and a man seated in the doorway. The black men who were carrying the hammock stopped there swearing that they would go no farther; but the gentlemen, fearing an ambush, said resolutely that we would continue the journey. Furious, the blacks hurled the hammock to the ground, and Mother du Rousier, who already ached all over from what she had undergone and because the position in which she was traveling was so uncomfortable, was injured even more by this shaking up. The blacks refused to take up their burden again, and threatened and blasphemed. They drew their knives, the gentlemen their pistols and we could tell they were going to go at it, when Don Joaquín Larraín, to stop the conflict, said that he and his brother would undertake to carry the hammock. But this declaration just seemed to increase the blacks' rage, until Don Ladislao, losing his patience, aimed his pistol at Encarnación, and she pointed her shotgun right back at him. Our Reverend Mother, lying on the floor, begged them to leave her there, and she asked for God's sake that Don Joaquín and the Colonel should abandon that disagreement which was so deadly for them all. Mr. Larraín decided then to ask for lodging in the cabin, where we were received with kindness by the black man who was in the doorway and was the owner. "These ladies are members of a religious order," said Don Joaquín, "and God will repay anything you may do for them." The old man gave a call in the door, and a woman and a girl came out bringing light, and we helped Mother du Rousier, who was lying on the ground in the hammock, to get up. We took her to a very small room separated from another larger one by a cane partition, and there she rested a bit on some bare boards, the only bed in the poor cabin. The gentlemen, who continued to be kind and caring, fixed a kind of mattress for her with their capes so that she would not be in such pain from her contusions. Mr. Larraín, using as pretext sending her shoes and stockings to be cleaned, carried them off and did that humble job all by himself. The daughter of the owner offered Mother MacNally her crude hammock, and it was accepted with gratitude even though it was very dirty.

Meanwhile they were fixing supper, and since this time we were allowed to eat in peace, our appetites rose to correspond to our prolonged fast, and we quickly ate the chickens they had just killed in our presence. Mother du Rousier was not able to get up and ate lying on her cross of rest. While we were eating, Encarnación, who truly was the incarnation of Satan and seemed to have decided not to leave us in peace for moment and was standing beside the table, blasphemed like a condemned person, sharpening her knife as though she were trying to scare us. When we had finished supper, our protectors took all possible precautions to get through the night in relative security, since they did not know if the owner of the cabin, who had received us so kindly, would be in league with Encarnación. Manuel, Mr. Herrera's black servant, armed with two pistols and a dagger, stretched out on the threshold of the entrance; the Colonel and Don Ladislao, also armed, sat on the floor leaning against the partition of our room, and Mr. Larraín, armed only with prayer, did the same thing. In spite of fatigue, no one closed an eye, knowing that we were surrounded with evildoers.

Suddenly we heard sounds and something like men's footsteps coming toward the cabin. We thought our last moments had come! The gentlemen stood up immediately, pistols in hand, and went to the door to call Manuel, and thanks be to God, it was just a false scare, because that noise was only the sound of our own mules walking over to us.

The night went by in a state of continuous alarm, and as soon as dawn began to break, we got ready to continue our journey. From our corner, we heard Mr. Larraín ask the woman of the house for water for the ladies and the black woman replied, gesturing to a tub, "There it is, white man, take it." With his accustomed thoughtfulness, he filled a gourd half full and brought it to us to refresh us; a little while later when we left our corner, I saw him kneeling beside the fire drying Mother du Rousier's stockings. I took them from him and while I finished drying them, he revived the fire, blowing with his mouth or waving air onto it with his hat, so that the coats hanging around the fire might dry.

Without any new incident, thanks to God, we continued our journey to Panama, and Encarnación, in exchange for a large sum, allowed us to take the hammock. When we arrived in the city we found the Canon Herrera with Don Manuel Irrázabal and all the members of the Peruvian Legation who had gone out to meet us. When they saw us, they evinced the greatest signs of delight; friends embraced very affectionately and, when we got to the inn, Sister Antonia came out to receive us with her arms open wide. She was extremely delighted to see us, since she had been afraid she would never see us again, and had spent the whole night praying and crying. It was eleven in the morning. They carried the hammock up to the third floor where they had prepared a very clean and well ventilated room with three beds for us. Mother du Rousier could hardly move, due to the effect of the blows and contusions she had received and the uncomfortable position she had been in while in the hammock. We spent all that day, Friday the 18th of August, resting and giving thanks to Our Lord. The misadventures of this trip made Reverend Mother du Rosier's virtue shine forth even more; as we have seen in her letter to the Reverend Mother of Limminghe, her soul was not distressed even by the fall down the precipice. No personal thought, no complaint could be heard from her even in the moments of greatest danger, and Mr. Larraín, who was expected to assess the virtue of the nuns he accompanied on their way to found an order new to Chile, could say upon arriving in Santiago, after having observed the Mother Superior closely, that during that long journey, he had not been able to discern any imperfection in her, or any womanly weakness: he had always seen the perfect nun.

She was thus sufficiently prepared to be a worthy instrument of God's great works.

OTHER NUNS COME TO JOIN ANA DU ROSIER IN 1854

On November 3, 1854, the first group of RSCJ sisters arrived in Santiago, via Cape Horn. They came to join the Santiago colony begun several months before by Ana du Rousier and her two companions. The new group was composed of the following: Thérèse du Lac, Joséphine Echeverría and Elisa Sieburgh, professed nuns; Isabel Plandiura and María Pujol, aspirants, and Marie Lenoir, novice. S. Magdalena Sofia sent them with her nephew, who was a priest, Abbot Dusausoy, because she could not permit her daughters to undertake such a perilous journey without assurance of the sacraments of the Church. This is the diary of that journey:

As we write to our venerated Mothers and to our dear sisters, first we need to express our gratitude for your many kindnesses to us and for the many prayers you have said on our behalf. But since total silence in regard to these matters has been imposed upon us, we will say only that we have felt their happy influence and we hasten to provide you with details about a journey which has otherwise been longer than it is interesting.

On Sunday, August 8 [1854] we went to the early mass at the Chapel of the Daughters of Charity, in Havre. When these ladies found out that we were about to embark, they prepared us a breakfast offered with the greatest cordiality. Their superior accompanied us to the pier, and around nine, we went on board the *Sirena*, a small brig that carried about thirty-two people, including the crew and fourteen passengers. They had prepared two cabins for us. One was occupied by our Worthy Mother du Lac and one of the ladies, and the other by the rest of the colony. We had not yet gotten ourselves settled when we felt the effects of the motion of the sea. We went up on the bridge: the weather was cold and misty; we watched the gradual fading away of the coast of France, where all that we most love is located: our most Reverend Mother General and the Center of our Society. Almost none of us got seasick during the first days; afterwards, only during some of the storms, but our worthy Mother has paid the toll for her daughters. Only during the last three weeks did she recover from seasickness, and the near impossibility of eating augmented her suffering. Nevertheless, she did not spend any entire day in bed.

The first difficulties we experienced were being becalmed in the English Channel and then the contrary winds which blew us toward the picturesque coast of Devonshire. There were a great many English fishing boats around and they often offered us fish in exchange for a little brandy. From the beginning, Our Lord gave us special signs of His protection. One night, the ship was about to hit a rock, and another night it nearly collided with a big English ship. It was so dark that there was barely time to avoid these dangers. On the 13th, we entered the Atlantic. The calm peaceful weather allowed tuna fishing, which was a new experience for us. On Assumption Day we had the happiness of hearing Mass and taking communion. This consolation was only allowed us three or four times during the crossing, since the Abbot Mr. Dusausoy obtained very restricted permission for these activities. The Captain invited the crew, and the seamen gathered in an adjoining room; a cabin boy assisted with the Mass and thanks to the foresighted charity of our Mothers, nothing was lacking to properly celebrate the Holy Sacrament. The Captain announced his intention of stopping in Madera, which pleased us very much, and we attributed this happy occurrence to the souls in Purgatory. At five o'clock on the 19th we saw the Porto Santo magpies, and a little after that, the deserted islands and arid rocks not far from Madera. Around noon we caught sight of Funchal, the main city on the island. We were just going to go visit it, when the wind blew us back to the high seas. The next day was Sunday and we were afraid that the Captain would decide to just go on. We would have given up this little excursion that we especially wanted to make in order to send our letters, but the need for water and fresh provisions made the Captain decide to make another try at landing on the island. After sunset, the city was illuminated little by little and sitting on the deck, we watched the fireworks display celebrating a holiday at the convent of La Merced. The rockets blended with the innumerable stars shining in the heavens. The air was serene and warm, it was a wonderful afternoon, appropriate for lifting one's soul to God. Unfortunately, our Worthy Mother could only enjoy it somewhat, and Madame Echeverría not at all, because they were both seasick. The following day, at six in the morning, *ma Mère* and three of our group went off in a boat under the command of the second Captain. We were more than a league offshore and he wanted to ask a Portuguese warship if we would be permitted to disembark. At this point the Governor of the island arrived in a covered launch and told us in French to follow him. He went to look for a doctor and for the port official. After he made certain that we did not have cholera, we disembarked, which was not easy because the beach was very steep. The launch was pulled to shore by many men, and we went directly to the French consul, Mr. Monteiro. Our affiliation with the Church is our best recommendation, so we were received very graciously. From there we went to the Cathedral where the parish priest said the Mass. We were impressed by the number of men who attended the Holy Sacrament, and by their profound devoutness. In contrast, the women were chatting and greeting each other whenever they wished. We also bought some blankets to protect ourselves from the cold of Cape Horn, and medications for our sick companions, after which we had lunch at a very well-kept hotel. Mesdames Echeverría and Lenoir joined us, but they arrived too late to hear Mass, so their guide took them to the convent of the Clarisas, where they were welcomed with tender charity. After showing them the Chapel and the inner choir, they took them to the reception room. The whole community came to the grille and although they spoke Portuguese, they could understand almost everything. They kissed Madame Echeverría's cross, they offered her a little basket full of sweets and flowers, making her promise to take it to the Mother Superior and the rest of the community. So we all went to the convent and they were very pleased. They have a school with forty girls. Many of them prefer to stay there on Sundays rather than return to their parents. They sell feather flowers made with an extraordinary naturalness and delicacy. Our Worthy Mother bought several of them from them. After promising each other to write, we left them regretfully and returned to the *Sirena*.

Except for Madera, the only other land we saw was the coast of Palma, one of the Canaries. However, gradually we began to feel the heat, and after we moved into the tropics, we began to enjoy the singular spectacle of flying fish. On several occasions they fell onto the bridge and they were fried for our Worthy Mother, who had such need of fresh food. Our Mothers know how beautiful tropical evenings can be. Sometimes we stayed out on deck until ten or eleven o'clock. They brought the harmonium up and our Worthy Mother and Madame Echeverría sang canticles and hymns. These religious songs reminded the Captain and his Assistant of the days of their childhood and the good principles that seem to have been instilled in them then. They often said to our Mother that these songs give faith. The Captain asked that they should be copied for him, and our Worthy Mother, taking advantage of his being well disposed, extracted at the end of the voyage the promise that he would pray to the Most Holy Virgin every day and that he would always wear a medal of the Immaculate Conception which she gave him. We even felt confident that he would return again to the sacraments.

Without doubt, Our Lord will reward this excellent seaman for his good care of the Brides of His Heart. Although the ship was small and uncomfortable, we were amply recompensed by the considerate attentions of Mr. Surmom and his Assistant.

We read together, and we said the Rosary prayers out loud. They never said an impolite word in our presence, and we never saw the seamen swear or fight. These gentlemen were all so well-behaved, we could feel right at home. Madame Planidura, faithful to her Sacred Heart religious mission, taught the catechism to the two cabin boys and the youngest seamen, teaching them prayers and saying the rosary with them. Our Worthy Mother concerned herself with making sure that they would go to Confession in Valparaíso. Madame Lenoir taught them reading and writing. Madame Echeverría gave a lesson in Spanish every day. We were able to pray, write, and work, so our small community in transit never suffered from boredom. The daughter of one of the second class passengers, a four or five year old child, spent a lot of time with us during our recreation periods. Her mother was very grateful to us. This poor woman, alone among so many men, suffered much more than we and was happy to entrust her little María to us.

The whole Society joined wholeheartedly in the celebration of our second Patron's Day thanksgiving. The Holy Sacrament was offered, to our great satisfaction. We had planned a festival to celebrate the Virgin Mary in the afternoon, but the rain interfered. However, Madame Planidura constructed a sort of tent, in which a beautiful image was hung. Four candle ends in our little drinking glasses lit it up for five minutes, while we sang a Magnificat. We think that the Most Holy Virgin would have liked this modest tribute, the only homage it was possible for us to offer externally.

During the first week of September, we had some very stormy days. There was so much, and such continuous, rain that we had to stay in our cabins. We celebrated the festival of the Holy Birth under the auspices of the Cross. We were all seasick, the storm went on and on, and we were not able to have a Mass. The winds carried us to the coasts of Africa, the water got into our cabins, and our Worthy Mother's bed was soaked. In the middle of the night, a big oil lamp that stood on the dining room table fell over and the oil spilled out. Since we had the "good luck" that this liquid as well as all the others around, ended up in our cabin, we were covered with oil. And we also had to get rid of three kittens that sought refuge with us.

Meanwhile, we saw all kinds of things pass by us: sharks, seamen, benches from galleys, and beautiful red fish that burn anything that touches them, so great precautions are necessary in order to catch them.

Our way of saying confession was quite picturesque: we used a shawl to make a partition in the biggest stateroom. The Abbot would slip furtively behind it, because we were always around in sight, and he would sit on a stool, since chairs were unheard of on the *Sirena*. The one confessing would sit or kneel on a trunk, depending on how hard the boat was rocking.

On the 15th and 16th we crossed the equator three times. That is, after we had crossed it once with a great deal of difficulty, the wind pushed us north and we had to circle around in order to avoid Penador Rock, which sticks up there. It was not until twenty four hours later that we crossed again into the southern hemisphere. For us, the Pole Star was replaced by the Southern Cross, a beautiful constellation we enjoyed pointing out in the sky. On Sunday morning, they performed the equator baptismal ceremony. The seamen put on grotesque disguises. Passengers who had not crossed the equator before were plunged into the water, getting wet from head to foot. It suffices to say that our condition as nuns saved us not only from any serious attempt, but even from the smallest jokes.

The 26th of September we received a new proof of the protection of the Heart of Jesus. They discovered that one of the masts was about to break, which would have caused serious damage to the prow. It took two whole days to replace the mast. Little by little we became aware of the change in temperature. In place of the oppressive heat of the tropics, the cold began to be felt sharply, and since the winds were pushing us to 59° in the southern latitude, we sometimes washed with melted snow. Water froze in pitchers, and since there was no stove on board, we were barely able to warm ourselves with a few jugs of hot water. This extreme cold only lasted two weeks. On the day of San Miguel, immediate preparations were begun for the fearful next step, hermetically sealing the windows of the cabins, which were thus left pretty dark, since they only received light from the deck.

From that point until its arrival in the bay of Valparaíso, the ship was constantly surrounded by quantities of black and white birds, about the size of ducks. They are commonly called *damiers cordonniers,* or cormorants. The first of October we saw a whale. Later we saw others, and near the Malvinas, one of those enormous cetaceans came to play near the ship, going past us again and again, just off the keel. Extreme cold kept us from enjoying this spectacle as long as we would have liked. The 6th of October we encountered a big ship from the United States going from Boston to California. The Captains asked each other various questions and compared their calculations of latitude and longitude, which were in agreement. Later on we would meet them again in Valparaíso. During this period, the winds were contrary. We were very busy preparing for the celebration of our Worthy Mother. We made a solemn novena to Saint Teresa to obtain relief from the bad weather. The pitching of the ship was so violent that it was impossible to do anything. The 14th, after lunch, we celebrated our Mother. We put on our religious habits, and the bigger cabin was covered in white. We had put up a kind of altar along the back wall. A "transparency," vases with painted cut-out flowers, the work of Madame Plandjura, various cardboard box arrangements, images that the Reverent Mother Desmarquest had given us and other simpler objects, made up the festive decorations, which made up in heart-felt devotion what they lacked in elegance. Madame Lenoir composed the music for the songs, and the next day we had more of a celebration. The party could not be kept secret from the Captain, and besides, he wanted to contribute to it. He ordered double rations given to the crew, and an extraordinary meal provided for the second class passengers, and to us he expressed his regret that the bad weather should have prevented the Abbot from saying Mass. Saint Teresa conceded us a few hours of good weather, but the next day the contrary winds returned and we were obliged to head for the Malvinas. We ran the risk of colliding with icebergs from the South Pole, but the Lord only wanted to test our faith. At the moment when we least expected it, the breeze became favorable and in twenty four hours we had gotten around Cape Horn, without the slightest danger. We were just joyfully anticipating the end of our trip when a last test moderated our impatience. The sea became very rough, and the winds blew violently. The Captain hoped that this would not last; since the ship was surrounded by *damiers*, the crew members occupied themselves fishing for these birds, which were extraordinarily good to eat. Big albatrosses began to appear. They caught eight of them, and the biggest had a wing span of nine feet. Their bodies are the size of a swan's; their feathers are brown and white. We tried to dissect one. If we can preserve it, our Worthy Mother plans to send it to Europe. The second Captain took advantage of all this to make several curious objects: with the feet he made pouches, with the bones, pipe stems, and with the skin, bed slippers.

Meanwhile, the storm got worse. The ship seemed to be in a hopeless state. They took down all the sails, stopped trying to steer it, and we gave ourselves up to the mercy of the tides or rather to the care of Providence. The waves were as high as mountains. Our fragile little boat went up and down on them. During five whole days we did not have one moment of rest. The waves broke on the deck with a terrifying sound. It was impossible to stand up. On the table, glasses, plates and silverware shifted around all mixed up. Our clothes, furniture, the floor: everything was flooded. We said novena after novena, we lit all the candles we had left, seeking comfort from the Most Holy Virgin. Our Worthy Mother made various promises to the souls in Purgatory. Finally the Heart of Jesus was moved, the storm ended, and on the 2nd of November we caught sight of the coast of Chile. The following day, at 11:30, we entered Valparaíso bay. A hundred ships of all nations were moored there.

The city is built like an amphitheater on low ridges. It would be difficult to describe the happiness we felt as we greeted this land, object of all our desires. Our Mother hoped to be able to leave on Monday for Santiago and she resolved to stay on board ship so as to avoid visits. In the afternoon, an agreeable surprise arrived: a letter from the Reverend Mother du Rousier. It told us that Monsignor had asked a Valparaíso family to prepare a room for us. Our Worthy Mother and two of our group went to thank Monsignor Salas for his thoughtfulness. We also went to visit a man in the city to whom Mother Serra had written to ask him to take charge of our baggage, but he had not received the letter. Monsignor Salas had foreseen everything: as we wished to spend a few moments at the feet of the Good Master and the churches were closed during the day, he took us to the convent of the ladies of Picpus (the Sacred Heart). These ladies received us with the greatest kindness and insisted that we stay with them. They showed us the chapel, the sitting room, the garden. Everything very well cared for. We admired the work of their students which was on display in the sitting room. They have 120 boarding students and 320 day students.

THE TRAVEL JOURNAL OF MME. JENDROLY
AND HER COMPANIONS, FROM HAVRE
TO SANTIAGO DE CHILE
(THE THIRD GROUP OF RSCJ NUNS TO TRAVEL TO CHILE)

February 23, 1857

My Most Reverend Mother,

Only today, the 16th of February, am I able to begin my little travel journal. The almost constant seasickness which has afflicted me since our voyage began, has not allowed me to take on any continuous task. Thus I am obliged to content myself with taking notes and writing them out more fully after I arrive in Santiago.

We set sail on the 5th of October of 1856 at around nine in the evening. The winds were so favorable, that we moved out of the Channel with extraordinary velocity, advancing 400 leagues in the amount of time it would usually have taken to travel 60 leagues, if we had not had that wind or if the sea had been very rough. For this reason, the Captain kept repeating that this astonishing speed at which we were moving along must be due to the prayers of the nuns who were passengers on the ship. But we attribute it to the many prayers on our behalf which are being said in our beloved convents in Europe, and especially in yours, my Most Reverend Mother, where none of your daughters is forgotten, however far away she may be! Good weather continued to favor us right up to the holy day of the Presentation. That day we had the first Mass. An altar had been set up on the deck, where a tent was erected. A banner announcing the celebration on shipboard of the Holy Sacrifice was displayed from the top of the mast. On this holy day, the nuns of the Good Shepherd renew their vows. They performed the ceremony in front of everyone present, despite the rain that began just as we had assembled for the Mass. It rained so heavily that it drenched the priest and threatened to put out the candles, despite the double layer of tenting hung over the altar. Since the priest had already gotten to the Offertory, he could not interrupt the Holy Eucharist. Because it was raining so hard, he asked for an umbrella, which had not occurred to anyone, and they brought him several. Despite the difficulties, these Sisters managed to renew their vows, which involves a much longer ritual than ours, during which time we were all truly on tenterhooks because of the weather. However, thanks to all the prayers, the rain diminished during the Elevation of the Host and stopped almost totally during Communion. As for me, I received two Hosts, since a drop of rain had stuck them together and even melted them a little. The priest had felt such great anxiety that he found himself quite indisposed for several days afterward. Around then we suffered our first delay of six to eight days, because the bad weather continued until we reached the equator. We sailed into the *pot-au-noir*, which is what they call the area around the equatorial line, and there we met up with more rain and unforeseen gales.

Finally we reached the equator on the first Sunday of Advent. The Captain made the announcement around one o'clock in the afternoon, and had barley water served to the ladies and beer to the men. There was no baptism out of consideration to us, but the seamen were given the freedom to do it. All the ladies were excused from this ceremony, but the gentlemen all got so wet, they had to change their clothes, even the priest.

The priest officiated at the second Mass the first Sunday of Advent. The weather was quite good, although a few drops of rain fell at the very end. I forgot to tell you about the songs at our first Mass at sea. Three Good Shepherd nuns, and Mr. Gubernatis and Mr. Dumont, provided the music. There were no instruments. At the beginning, they sang "Toujours," and for the Elevation of the Host, "Venez, Jésus." The first Sunday of Advent they sang "Venez divin Messie" and "O Salutaris." As for the holy observance of the other Sundays on the ship: we did not work, and the priest and we nuns sang Vespers at two thirty. Following Vespers there was a short sermon by the priest, to which the better part of the passengers came. On ordinary days, the Father provided the spiritual lesson, as well as morning and evening prayers.

I have still not told you anything about the crew, my Most Reverend Mother, and they deserve a paragraph. The Captain, a good man, bestowed a great deal of attention and many kindnesses on the passengers, and especially on us, the nuns. He practices religion, as do the sailors. That is: he is very devoted to the Most Holy Virgin and he often invokes her. He told us that he never takes off his holy medal, and we offered him one of the Immaculate Conception, which he immediately hung around his neck on a cord. He likes hymns very much, and sometimes he sang along with us. He was the first to order that all should be prepared for the celebration of the Holy Eucharist, and he came to that service. He also took care not to say crude words in front of us, swear words which are so common to sailors. The first mate also showed us his medal with pride, and the whole crew asked us for one, and each one received it with true devotion. Counting the crew and the passengers, there were twenty people, besides the nuns. They all conducted themselves so well that we suffered no displeasure on that hand. Nor were we too uncomfortable in our clothing due to the heat.

The day of the Immaculate Conception was the best day of our entire voyage. Holy Mass was celebrated while it was perfectly calm, and we were all able to gather. During the Holy Eucharist, they sang a hymn to the Immaculate Virgin, an "O Salutaris," and during the Prayer of Thanksgiving, all of the children: five little girls between six and eight years old, and two little boys, one of then aged two and a half—the plaything of all the passengers—dressed in white, pledged their Consecration to the Virgin, which was very well read by one of the little girls. Then the priest blessed the medals of the Immaculate Conception and gave them to the children, saying some appropriate words to them as he did so. The medals hung from blue cords and all of them, especially the necks of the little ones, were proud to wear them. The little ceremony ended with some couplets to the Most Holy Virgin. At two thirty, we sang Vespers. Immediately afterward, the priest gave one of his most beautiful sermons in honor of the Immaculate Virgin. In the evening, the Captain set off some very curious fireworks: they consisted of two kegs of tar and fish oil set afire, floating on the sea. They looked like two fireballs; it was a truly beautiful sight. The magnificently starry sky, the calm sea, the singing of the

Magnificat: everything contributed to fill our hearts with emotion and provide a favorable impression. However, right after this beautiful day, we suffered through many dismal weeks.

On the 19th of December we underwent the first danger. A storm broke over us with no warning. The lightning conductors were not set in place, and the Captain turned white as a sheet of paper. We began to pray the rosary out loud, and thanks to the Most Holy Virgin, we were freed from the terror which affected the Captain so, that he was extremely indisposed for several days. This storm surprised us in La Plata, where ships are often subject to some dangers. It was there, also, that the winds remained contrary for eight days, which meant that it was New Year's before we approached Cape Horn. Despite the bad weather and the continuous pitching of the ship, which rocked back and forth endwise and kept making us seasick, we had the happiness of celebrating a Christmas Eve Mass. The altar was set up inside the ship. On one side, the Good Shepherd sisters arranged a small crèche scene. The different-sized dolls represented Jesus, Mary and Joseph. All of us, without exception, got involved in dressing them. For my part, I made crocheted lace to trim Baby Jesus' little shirt. All of us nuns spent the night in prayer and preparations. Most of the passengers and the children had gone to bed. The children appeared at the Christmas Eve Mass all dressed in white, and arranged themselves near the crèche scene. Two of the gentlemen helped with the Mass. They sang the canticle of the shepherds: "Gloria," "Et Verbum," the old version, and the "Adeste." After the Elevation of the Host, they drew a kind of veil or curtain across the manger scene to hide it, and during the Prayer of Thanksgiving, they intoned "Il este né..." The Captain had a Christmas Eve supper served, but only Sister Dolores was able to eat anything. We all went to bed right away. Christmas day was tiring because of the pitching of the ship. The bad weather stayed with us, but finally we caught sight of Cape Horn, which would afford us so many bad days.

But before I go on, I need to give you a description of how we managed Confession. Most Reverend Mother: altogether we had five Confessions, five Masses and five Communions during these three months. The Captain loaned us his room for the confessions. There we hung a black cloth between a sofa and a table, so the confessor and the penitent could sit one on either side. The preparations were made amidst all the conversations and the games of the passengers and children. The last day of the year, the four of us recited the "Miserere" and the "Te Deum." We made up all of our disagreements and all embraced each other in peace. All this went on in our cabin where—because it was so small—the four of us could barely squeeze in. For this reason, we had set up four sets of different times to get up and go to bed, since it was impossible for all of us to undress or dress at the same time.

On New Year's Day, the dinner was splendid. The passengers wished the Captain a happy year and sang some appropriate songs, but the bad weather deprived us of the happiness of celebrating a Mass and the whole month of January was without sacraments. On February 2nd, a big storm worried us seriously. A gust of wind destroyed two sails. All of the passengers pitched in to help and we nuns again appealed to the Most Holy Virgin reciting the rosary out loud while the danger lasted. The night was most distressing due to the incessant rocking of the ship from side to side, tipping our beds so that we were in danger of falling out. The next day, the sea was calm and we could see Tierra del Fuego. If the wind had continued to be favorable for us, we would have gone around Cape Horn on the 6th of January, and could have reached Chile on the 15th. But we barely reached the Islas de los Estados, because contrary winds kept blowing. We had to put about and turn back and return to where we had been up to three times a day, and often during the night, too. The direction of the winds changed continuously, and along with this, the temperature changed, so you could say we experienced all four seasons in a single day. But for three consecutive weeks it was extremely cold, and we had snow, hail and ice. We had to put on wool camisoles, shawls, mittens, and boots. And despite all this, we suffered a lot with chilblains. One of our little children had his hands covered with them.

During twenty-three long days, the only question you could hear as you left your cabin was: "Is the wind going to change?" And always the answer: "Not the most contrary wind, the one that forces the ship back." Ah! I have to add to this, my Most Reverend Mother, that patience and prayer were more than necessary. Finally, the priest proposed saying a novena to the blessed Pedro Claver. We did this, but after nine days, there still were no changes. We only asked for the bad weather to improve and in this sense we were listened to, because after twenty three days of battle at Cape Horn—and some ships had to wait for forty-five days, or even for two months—a favorable wind allowed us to go around it on January 24th. There was general happiness, and the faces were joyful and everyone was more lively and cordial than ever before. On the 25th we entered the Pacific Ocean. It appears more grandiose and agreeable than the Atlantic. But we had various days of calm which delayed us.

Our last Mass took place on February 2nd, also on a holy day of the Most Sainted Virgin. It was a beautiful, calm day. The sea had never looked so beautiful. That day we saw some whales, several porpoises and hundreds of albatrosses. The latter are aquatic with long necks and rosy coloring. Their wings are black and white striped. They are the size of a swan and the seamen catch them like they catch fish. They caught at least five or six and we saved the feet, a head, and many feathers as curiosities. On the 24th of February, the rocking and tipping of the ship affected us for a last time, and the day was unpleasant.

But the 5th of March, what joy! We spotted land!!! That was at five in the morning and by around seven, we were already alongside Valparaíso. At nine o'clock the priest and we nuns sang the Magníficat and the Laudate on the deck. We had breakfast on board and disembarked around eleven in the morning. The priest was the first to go find the Damas de Picpus [nuns of the Sacred Heart] who had a very attractive establishment in Valparaíso. He came back to say that those good sisters were waiting for us. We got into a small launch and after more or less ten minutes, we stepped out onto dry land. It is impossible to describe to you how overwhelmed with happiness we felt, my Reverend Mother. You have to have been sailing on the sea for five months, exposed to continuous dangers and uncertainties, to privations of all kinds, especially in what concerns the religious life, in order to understand what one's soul feels seeing itself at the feet of the Most Holy Sacrament, taking deep breaths of silence, solitude, etc. These nuns have been very good to us. The Mother Superior has expressly asked me, my Most Reverend Mother, to tell you from her that from now on we should be sure to send her our newly arriving sisters, because here it is unheard of for nuns to stay in a hotel. The Damas de Picpus offer hospitality to foreign nuns, and men who are in orders go stay with the Padres de Picpus.

As soon as we had arrived, the Archbishop, who was in

Valparaíso for a dedication ceremony, called us. He received us very benevolently and informed us of the indisposition of Reverend Mother du Rousier. She has been seriously ill, but thanks be to God she is now well. We found ourselves obliged to prolong our stay in Valparaíso because of our baggage. After we had disembarked, a gust of wind broke the ship's chains, even though it was anchored. It was hurled against another ship and both of them were damaged. The losses are estimated at 10,000 francs. We recovered all of our suitcases, with the exception of the one containing the books. Nevertheless, we hope that they will be able to recover it from the bottom of the hold. The Good Shepherd sisters left on the 9th in coaches provided by the Government. Reverend Mother du Rousier informed us by way of Monseñor, that she wished us to leave with a priest, the chaplain of the hospital, a French priest entirely dedicated to those who are newly arrived, the same one who took Mother du Lac to Santiago. He hastened to offer us his services.

He said Mass for us at four in the morning, but we had to wait until one o'clock in the afternoon for the coach, following the custom of the country. We were obliged to seek lodgings along the road. The little house where we stopped was passable enough. After spending a good night, we got back on the road at five in the morning. We still had to cross over the highest mountains. You have to switch back and forth thirty times before reaching the summit. The roads are quite wide, but they are right along the edge of precipices. In addition, the coaches do not stop during the descent, which the coachmen make with a speed unheard of in Europe. At first it is terrifying, but then one is reassured by the driver's confidence and skill. Accidents rarely happen. We were only troubled by the incredible clouds of dust, which can be explained by the dryness and the negligence with which the roads are maintained.

The streets of Santiago seem interminably long, but that is necessitated by the frequent earthquakes.

We reached our beloved Sacred Heart at ten thirty. The first person we saw was the worthy Mother Dulac. She seemed to me as good and as cordial as ever, but so thin. A moment later the Reverend Mother du Rousier appeared, and received us with an entirely maternal tenderness. As soon as we entered, don Salvo, the aged priest so loved by our Mothers, came to offer to say a Mass of Thanksgiving for us the next day. We celebrated the Mass with music and the joy of receiving Holy Communion. The rest of the day we spent at leisure. Friday and Saturday were also days of recreational gatherings, since these nuns entered into seclusion on Saturday evening.

On those days we did some substituting for our Sisters at the Normal School, which has fifty-four girls enrolled. They never go out during their stay at the Sacred Heart. Our house has the look of a true Nazareth: everything about it speaks of saintly poverty. But the Chapel, which is the best room of the house, is decorated with much good taste and even with true elegance, thanks to the industry of the worthy Mother Dulac and gifts from some of our convents in Europe. The students of the Normal School are in charge of the songs, fruit of Mother Dulac's zeal. She does not rest even on holy days. Here the vacation lasts until March 2nd.

We four are lodged for the moment in the old infirmary, converted into a future dormitory for novices. There are two Choir Novices here now, one a student and Daughter of Mary, the first of our boarding students to feel the vocation. The other, a postulant, is a young woman who is a close relative of Monseñor, the Archbishop. She is a distinguished person, but her family is putting up many obstacles to her entering the order. In our dormitory there is akind of pedestal on which there is set a statue of the Most Holy Immaculate Virgin, surrounded by bouquets of lilies. Above her there hangs a medallion with the image of Saint Estanislao. The pedestal is made out of a box which is its base; the pedestal under that is a barrel of sugar. Both of them are covered with a gray-painted cloth. This is an example of the ingenuity exercised by our mothers. At every step we find these instances of their industry. However, the present building will no longer suffice, because students must be turned away now because of lack of room.

Our health has not been affected by all the sufferings we underwent during our journey. At the moment we are all very well, though in the future we may pay tribute to the country's climate. Our Worthy Mothers du Rousier and Dulac have been cruelly tried by illnesses. They suffer from them almost continually, but whenever the opportunity for sacrifice presents itself, they are most selfless and most generous. I am profoundly impressed by the virtue I see them practice and I feel a strong desire to be granted the grace to walk in their footsteps. It must be their prayers, my Most Reverend Mother, which confer this remarkable grace upon the lowliest of their daughters. I often reread your precious letter and try to follow your counsels. Allow me to recommend myself to the kind memory of the Reverend Mothers Desmarquest, Henriette and Prévost, to all my Mothers and Sisters of the Motherhouse, and to our Probationary Sisters.

There is much good that can be done here, but we will only accomplish it through virtue. You know, my Most Reverend Mother, how deficient in virtue your poor daughter is. I beseech you to bless her and commend her to the Sacred Hearts of Jesus and Mary, so that she may be less unworthy of the small mission the Lord will entrust to her devoted obedience.

My greatest desire is to be able to ultimately show myself as totally dedicated, truly religious and to thus demonstrate, my Most Reverend Mother, how I value the grace of having been admitted into our beloved Society where I can work for the glory of the Sacred Hearts of Jesus and Mary.

I remain, with sentiments of the most profound respect and the most intense gratitude, as

Your very submissive daughter
Marie Amélie Jendroly
Residence of the Sacred Heart

Marie Amélie Jendroly was born in Vienna on May 25, 1815, daughter of Louis Jendroly, Inspector of the House of Regency of Vienna. She took the habit on April 4, 1842 and made her religious profession on August 27, 1848. She arrived in Chile on March 5, 1857 and died in 1862 in the Sacred Heart community in Talca.

SACRED HEART NUNS FOUND NEW CONVENTS: TALCA (1858) AND CONCEPCIÓN (1865)

Talca

A previous journey to Talca and the departure of the founding nuns may be found in Volume I of the Diario de Maestranza:

1858, October 4. The worthy Mother du Lac and Madame Valdivieso leave us to go spend two weeks in Talca. The journey was fraught with misfortunes. Heading south from San Fernando the only transportation they could find was in a rickety cart with ailing horses. They spent the nights in wretched huts that served as inns, where enormous rats interrupted what little rest they were able to get, seated on little chairs and in the freezing cold.

1858, November 22. Departure of the colony of founders. Our schoolgirls, who possessed great vivacity of emotion, expressed their grief in a moving way when they first witnessed the departure of their teachers, who had dedicated themselves so earnestly to instructing them well.

> Volume I of the Diario de Talca (1858 to 1881) relates the journey from Santiago to the foundation of Talca. This part of the diary is written in Spanish, in the orthography prescribed by Andrés Bello's grammar:

We left Santiago the day after the Presentation of the Blessed Virgin, the 22nd of November of 1858 at eight o'clock in the morning. The first day would have gone quite well, had it not been for the extreme discomfort of one of our sisters who became totally nauseated by the jolting carriage, so much so that it was necessary to almost carry her in order to cross the seven rivers our road crossed. The rivers were very high due to the melting snow, and in these circumstances, in order to facilitate crossing the rivers, an unusual kind of bridge is constructed: two heavy chains are anchored to twelve great posts on either side of the river, and between these chains a thin path of willow twigs is interwoven with ropes. They call it a suspension bridge, since it sways a lot, and looking down, you can see the water through the chinks. The carriages are pulled across by hand, the luggage is carried on men's backs, while the travelers creep along on uncertain feet. At night we stopped at the hacienda of one of our sisters, where they welcomed us with the most cordial hospitality. The following morning we heard Mass in the domestic chapel with music played by the young ladies of the house. The second stop took place in Curicó, where the Señor Cura had offered us lodging, but through miscommunication, he did not expect us so soon. We found ourselves obliged to stay at the home of an individual who came forward to receive us very graciously, but it is impossible to describe the disorder that reigned there. After many comings and going on the part of the charitable woman, who kept apologizing profusely, we were ushered into a room that did not seem to have seen a broom for a long time. An enormous bed in the back of the room had a complete man's outfit draped around it as curtains: overcoat, pants, jacket, shirt, and under the bed were the boots and a little farther off, a hat. The dusty furniture was covered with a thousand objects scattered about in disorder. It took a very long time to sort through such chaos and to finally be able to arrange the enormous mattress so that we could go to bed. The Holy Mass and Communion we received the next day in Curucó made us easily forget the trivial irritations of the previous day.

We began our third day, which culminated in the most incredible reception. Around six o'clock we reached the Lircay River, not far from Talca, and after we had ordered our carriage stopped, we sent a messenger to advise them of our arrival. Soon afterward we saw him return armed with an enormous feather duster with which he began to brush off the carriage with such energy that he damaged our toilette, the disorder of which we had just repaired, A.M.D.G. [for the greater glory of God]. Just after that, the venerable Cura Tapia made his appearance, with other ecclesiastical dignitaries and the important people of the town, who all expressed their satisfaction very eloquently. Eighteen to twenty carriages full of ladies followed this first delegation. The ladies took charge of us, overwhelming us with affection. They galloped along the road to the city right to the Parish Church where military music awaited us. The regular and secular clergy came out to meet us. The plaza commander tried in vain to contain the crowd that burst through the military ranks. With great difficulty we managed to enter the Church and go up to the Main Altar, where His Divine Majesty was displayed. There, they gathered us in a half circle, and meanwhile the *Tedeum* was entoned. The Señor Cura, deeply moved, addressed us with a speech interrupted by his tears, in these terms: "I am not the Angel who in an earlier time proclaimed the coming of the Savior of nations, but I am here to announce to you that these are terrestrial Angels who have left distant shores to...etc."

You can imagine our situation among such effusions of enthusiasm. When the speech was over, they accompanied us to the Sacred Heart house, with the bells pealing and military music playing, amidst a huge crowd. The streets were decorated with triumphal arches, and private homes were adorned. When we stepped out of the carriage, they almost suffocated us by crowding in to kiss our rosaries and holy medals. A large number of women were waiting for us in the entrance patio, where they covered us with flowers and led us to the indoor chapel to take part in the blessing of the Most Holy. When we returned to the salon, they served us refreshments and we even had to eat dinner in public. Finally the visitors disbursed, little by little. But, to give an idea of the patriarchal simplicity that gleams here in all its splendor, one of the Señor Cura's pious friends showed us to our rooms, and thinking that the beds were not properly made, he straightened them out, much to our great embarrassment.

The founders of Talca were: Thérese du Lac (French), Josephine Lliros (Spanish) and Nieves Squella, Mercedes Gaete and Matilde Ladrón (Chilean). Except for Mother du Lac, the Superior, the others were all postulants.

CONCEPCIÓN

Volume I of the Diario de Maestranza relates the 23rd of March of 1865:

The departure of Mother MacNally for the foundation of Concepción, with Mothers Prats, Blount, Valdivieso, Irene Armas and Sister Javiera. Our Reverend Mother Vicar, since she is still much affected by a head cold, received the travelers privately and was not able to preside over the General Farewell. The worthy Mother MacNally, who arrived twelve years ago with the Reverend Mother du Rousier to begin the Work of the Sacred Heart in Chile, leaves behind in this house, as well as sorrow for her departure, the example of her religious spirit and the memory of her boundless devotion.

Volume I of the Diario de Concepción (1865-1883), records on its first pages:

The year 1865. Our Reverend Mother General and founder, ceding to the reiterated pleas of Monseignor Salas, Bishop of Concepción, permitted our Reverend Mother du Rousier to begin the foundation of a House in Concepción. The Worthy Mother MacNally, named Superior, left Santiago on the 24th of March of 1865 with a small colony composed of three nuns from the choir: M. Pratz, Margarite Blount, Irene Armas and one professed Sister.

The Concepción newspaper, *La Tarántula*, reported on the reception the nuns received upon their arrival in that city:

MARCH 26, 1865. March 26, 1865 will always be a memorable day for the city of Concepción, and the annals will conserve the record! The Bishop, together with his worthy clergy and the city's most important citizens, awaited this day with fervent anticipation, because he had already received the news that the steamship that came from Valparaíso to Talcahuano would bring the nuns of the Sacred Heart of Jesus, for the purpose of founding in Concepción one of those prized educational establishments which are so renowned for inculcating moral and cultural values, in whatever town they exist, and which have a highly deserved reputation for excellence all over the world. From the city, a committee named by the Bishop, composed of the Archdeacon Don Mateo Jara, the Penitenciary Canon Don Domingo Benigno Cruz, and Father Don Vicente S. Chaparro, departed to go receive the nuns. As soon as the ship, called the *Guayaquil*, dropped its anchor in port, this honorable committee went down to the pier to welcome the nuns and accompany them to the city. When they had disembarked, they all headed for the Church to give thanks to God and hear the Holy

Mass. During the Holy Sacrifice, skillful hands played soft music on an excellent harmonium. After the Mass, two ladies from the first ranks of society, resident in Talcahuano, Doña Rosa Esquella de Serrano and Doña Carmen Serrano de Moller, and an eager crowd of followers, accompanied the nuns to the house prepared for them. Everyone admired their bearing and their edifying modesty.

At the house, a splendid luncheon awaited them. It was served with that amiable cordiality which characterizes our upper class ladies. The eminent Don Horacio Serrano, his wife and his sister proved themselves eminently worthy of their high social position. Their refined manners and their piety, for which they are renowned, rank them among the most distinguished members of our society. After lunch, Mr. Chaparro thanked the Serrano family, in the name of the Bishop, for the cordial welcome they had arranged for the nuns.

At ten thirty in the morning, the nuns stepped into the stagecoach, followed by several gentlemen. During the entire journey from the port to the city—a four hour trip—they were the recipients of fervent welcoming greetings. From time to time they had to stop the stagecoach to receive the greetings and congratulations of the families that assembled along the road to meet the nuns. They all clamored for the honor of transporting one of the nuns in their own coaches. The first to present himself was the distinguished gentleman, Don Miguel Prieto. Next came the Méndez Urrejola family, which stopped the stagecoach to carry the Mother Superior off in their own carriage. A few steps later, the distinguished Minister of the Court of Appeals, Don Domingo Ocampo and his sister, Doña Rosa, in company with the Archdeacon, eagerly awaited the convoy. A little bit farther it was stopped again by Doña Josefa Zañartu de Cruz and her daughter, Miss Delfina Cruz de Pinto. Finally, at the entrance to the city, the ladies Doña Zacarías Urrutia de Eguiguren and Doña Domitila Rosas de Urrutia also approached the stagecoach and each of these families invited one of the nuns to ride in their coaches. Thus they made their entrance into the city amidst the joyous clamoring and applause of the populace.

These carriages and others, as well, that awaited the newly arrived nuns, rolled along the streets and the coachmen, with their triumphant airs and cracking horsewhips, seemed to invite the passersby to take part in this universal celebration. In effect: everyone looked out of their doors and windows with an expression of intense joy on their faces. The bells of the churches began to ring, and banners waved from all the bell towers. When the coaches drew up in front of the comfortable and beautiful house that the Bishop had had prepared for the nuns' residence and educational establishment, a large group of people of all social classes poured into the house as well as crowding the street. The Bishop in ceremonial robes, the Seminary Director and the Rector, attired in choir robes, accompanied by their acolytes, received the nuns processionally and took them to the chapel of their house.

The Bishop, seated on his throne, was on the right hand side. The Mother Superior was placed near "Sa Grandeur." Around them were the clergy and several people from the Magistrate's office. The other nuns were seated on the left with several ecclesiastical dignitaries.

* * *

TRIP TO CHILE, 1874

One day in Santiago, our Reverend Mother du Rousier called me into her chambers; I hurried there with eagerness, with a big heart, for she was leaving in a few days to visit the houses of the Vicar, and I did not doubt that she did not want, in her motherly kindness, to give me her last advice before her departure. This was therefore a joy since she said these words to me, "I need a travel companion and thought about taking you with me, since you are the most useless in the house." I thanked our Lord, at least this time, with all of my heart for being useless, and at the same time promised him, that with his grace, I would try both during and after the voyage, to make myself as useful as I could in recognition of this opportunity. And, in order to share my joy, I thought about writing a diary for my reverend mothers in Europe, containing descriptions as well as sketches of my trip to Chile, a place where art has already done some destruction to the beauties of nature, and to facilitate the traffic of the habitants. But these charms will shortly end, for in a few years, one will be able to travel in countries in Europe, as due to the growth of the railroads. I would especially like to bring the obeying grace, love for our Lord, and devotion back to our society, for without these incentives, I am strongly persuaded that the Reverend Mother du Rousier will never in her age tolerate such travels in the future.

November 30

After having adorned and asked our good Sister Narcisa and I, we left our dear family in Santiago and arrived at our first stop, Curicó. The train was composed of Americans; it was hot and every once and a while a waiter passed, offering ice to the passengers. As for me, the beauty of the countryside stops me from suffering neither from the heat, nor from fatigue, because I have full permission to use my eyes as I want, in addition, my mother asks me every once and a while if I have seen everything; oh, yes, nothing escapes me and I do not get tangled up in my admiration. To our left, we have the vast mountain range named the Cordilières, where the white woodpeckers contrast the bright blue in the sky; to our right, there are smaller mountains; the valley is sometimes wide-spread, then it closes until the point where the two end mountains seem to touch, and is then ready to open again, smiling more than ever; it is absolutely ravishing...the vast fields of wheat, the prairies inhibited by hundreds of horses, the ox with their long horns, the calves, and the sheep...sometimes the farms are well cared for by their proprietors, one floor in elevation, surrounded by a gallery and often by a beautiful garden...it is all delightful.

At the stations, I see men riding horses, with their big *sombrero*, their brightly-colored *poncho*, their umbrella made of ostrich feathers, their massive stirrups made of sculptured wood, and even of silver, if they are wealthy; in hand a long pike or a gun...their entire appearance is as picturesque as possible, even the suiting of their horses, because men and women, rich and poor, are accustomed from an early age to this livelihood. The horses are small, lively, and fast, they are also quite beautiful when properly taken care of. At one station, I admire one's view of freedom, equality, and brotherhood in Chile, for in a shadow, under a tree just big enough to shelter them, I see a cat, dog, pig, and woman, living in perfect harmony! The homes of the poor have a miserable quality. There is a pile in each corner to which there are attached some bamboo canes covered in mud, forming the bedroom, it is without windows and has a small sort of roof made out of bamboo. These habitations, miserable as they are, suffice the needs of a country where there are no storms and rarely any rain.

Around 7 o'clock we arrived in Curicó, the owner of the hotel greeted us and drove us; ah! what a carriage, it was mounted quite high over the tires...to get into it one needed Jacob's ladder; my Mother was used to all kinds of graces, that, however, are not easy, even for people who are still agile...we finally arrived, and the innkeeper with us, the three horses left trotting off despite the terrible state of the road: it was half paved and filled with big holes and stones. The houses are only one-story, and the most upkept are painted in blue starch, as our hotel is, where we have a bedroom which is relatively clean, containing three beds. Before going to sleep, the innkeeper told us that we would be accompanied by gentlemen in the carriage tomorrow; this did not please us too much, and we prayed for the good souls in Purgatory to change this.

December 1

After Curico, there were no more railroads, so at 8:30 we took a carriage for Talca, we stopped at noon at Molina, at the house of Pepa, former student of *L' Ecole Normale Supérieure*, who having come this year to Santiago to retire, prayed for my Mother to come to her house in Molina so that she would make her visits in the Curacy. The carriage perched high, like the one from yesterday, has no windows; in order to close it, one must hammer a morsel of leather over opening. The mechanism interests me, it is composed of a piece of raw wood, at least six inches in diameter. We depart at a gallop, for it is the style; the horses in the name of five are harnessed side by side with a line, they are the best in the world, and stop for nothing; the coachman never uses a whip, a small whistle is enough, and the more the road is unkept the faster they go, to overcome, without doubt, the difficulties, such as the holes, ditches, and large rocks, which in Europe are classified as in surmountable; we pass the torrents in the same manner...the jolts are terrible, one always needs to grasp on to the carriage in order to avoid being thrown around on one another, for the bumps continued without interruption. I look at my Reverend Mother with shock. How can she tolerate this. As she is laughing, she looks at me and says: "What would one think of such a trip to Europe, and nevertheless, it is nothing compared to what it used to be!" There aren't any true public roads in Chile, only paths naturally formed by the continual passage of carts, etc. Every now and then we sink into deep sand, and more often we only follow the dry bed of a stream, other times it would look like we go haphazardly, through a field. After an hour, we approach the big Rio Lontué, one of Chile's largest stream; it is about three to four miles in width. When the snow melts in the Andes, this expanse is under water; right now, it is divided into several more or less strong and deep currents, in which our carriage and horse immerses itself in a full gallop, dispersing water to the right and to the left, and dislocating our poor bones...now, I understand the reason why the carriages are set in a high place, it is necessary so that the water does not enter into the interior.

At last, we arrive at the main current, we get out of the carriage because we have to walk across one of the most original and primitive bridges I have ever seen! Two chains, suspended from large tree trunks, blackened by fire, are thrown from one edge to the other, strong bamboo is linked together by large and thick straps of hide au naturel in a way that the cow's hide can be seen, some were black, others were red, others were white, etc.; these straps are in turn attached to the chain and this forms a suspended bridge that is 500 feet long and wide enough so that three people can cross it together. It is difficult to keep one's balance, because the bamboo underneath one's feet is not solid and the bridge, which is crooked, dances with each step. There is a tradition; the first time that the dignified Mother Sieburg crossed the bridge, she knelt down in the middle to perform an act of contrition to prepare herself for death, and to commend her soul to God! I give my Mother my arm, and we begin our journey, while we detach our trunks and transport them on our shoulders to the other edge. Our attention is drawn to four pairs of oxen who swim across the current a little further up than where the bridge is. They have the yoke on their necks and are linked together; a man on the first pair and another on the last pair, guide them. It is nice to see their black heads that come out of the water. Shortly, they make a violent effort to resist the current, but are carried away without success...the first two oxen are turned over, feet in the air, the head below; the men have trouble holding themselves up on these poor animals...they rapidly approach the bridge, where we find ourselves halfway across. The water is only five or six feet beneath us, they pass very close to us like a flash of lightning, and give us a desperate look that I will never forget; Oh Jesus! Have pity on them! One man disappears, we throw a lasso into the current in hopes that he could grab it. At last, seven or eight hundred feet further down, they are thrown on to shore, but one man is missing. "Where is he?" we anxiously ask, because no one seemed to worry about him. We were given a laconic reply: *Se fue* (he disappeared). "But where?" we ask once again. "To the bottom." Yes, he drowned! No one is interested, it is useless, they say, because there are so many holes in the bed of the current that we would never find him. Our Father, without a doubt, in his mercy, permitted this misfortune to happen in our presence so that we would pray for him!

Our coachman, who is a prudent man, takes the time to look for a reliable ford to cross the stream. We have to wait an hour and a half before it arrives to us. During this time, we take cover from the sun's rays under a roof of branches called *ramada*. My Mother can sit on a tree trunk and me, I make a few sketches of our surroundings. I see things that are new to my eyes and that interest me immensely. First, a big mean bull who scares everyone, we have to make him cross the bridge. The men skillfully throw their lassos around his horns and feet, so as to make him fall. They keep him in this position until the bridge is clear, then, let the ropes go a little, the poor animal thinks it is liberated, he jumps up on to his feet and starts to run, but he is with-held by the man behind him and by one who is ahead of him. A quarter of an hour passes as they struggle to make him cross the bridge. Next, a beautiful man arrives in a *sombrero* and *poncho*, white like snow, silver stirrups, and a charming little black horse who is too well mannered to dare to put his feet on the bridge...at last, he. advances with delicate little steps, after lots of caresses from his master. The men come over to ask my Mother for some medals, she has a large provision; I like to see these good people, darkened by the sun, simply come close to my Mother! Finally, here is the carriage; we abandon our intention to stop at Pepa's because our Mothers in Talca will be worried because of the delay. We will simply tell them why.

We then stopped in Molina; Pepa, the radiant figure, runs to open the door. My Mother tells her that we cannot get out...poor Pepa, she is inconsolable. She begs so well that my Mother cannot resist and we enter the house and we visit the establishment. Pepa runs a school, for 150 children from the countryside, founded by a woman to teach them not only to read and write, but also things related to housekeeping. The dormitories, the refectory, everything is poor but clean. Holy Mass is given every day in the little chapel. Next to the altar, there is a statue of the Holy Virgin; she is in all of her glory, because it is Mary's month in Chile; red cheeks, black curly hair, a bellying out blue dress...my poor good Mother, can we treat you this way!!

We take to the road again, and from time to time, we change horses who leave to the neighboring prairie, while we catch others with the lasso. The process is a bit long and primitive, we take off the harnesses from the horses. During these stops, I gather bouquets of flowers appropriate for the lounge of a king.

During some hours, we cross a big uncultivated and dry plain, in the meantime, I like this wild beauty, and we still have the beautiful white mountains in the distance, where one, higher than the others is called *Descabezado,* cut-off head; it is an ancient extinct volcano. We follow for a while the deep but large gully, dug by the Rio Claro, that has banks that are covered by magnificent trees, in which numerous groups of big parrots flutter. Later on, we go down the steep sides of the gully to pass the ford of the river. We stop at the edge so that a man with his wife on his back, has the time to get to the other side. My Mother says that our Father, who loves to please by doing little things, permitted this comic scene to happen because in all of her trips, she has never seen such a thing. The woman is big, the passage long, the current strong, and the man, who holds a cudgel in his hand to support himself, only has one arm to hold his beloved; little by little, he lets her slide backwards, until it looks like she is sitting on the water, while her legs ascend; she does not worry, but once on land she shakes the water from her clothes, content with herself and her husband.

After this, my Mother, who is very tired and indisposed, continuously vomits. She can not rest for an instant, because the road is the worst it has ever been. Oh! It hurts to see her suffer without being able to do anything to relieve her! In the meantime, she is energetic and self-sacrificing as always...even during her vomiting she finds a way to tell me the name of the river that we are crossing, and as she is laughing, she looks at me, when there is the worst jolt thus far. I thank our Father for having saved this trip with this venerated Mother, it is the renunciation and self-forgetfulness personified, and since I am from this probation that carries this name, I am touched and I take advantage to make practical resolutions for the proper conduct.

Around 6 a.m. we arrive in Talca; though one of the main cities in Chile, it does appear like one because the one story houses look shabby. We get down at our dear Convent. After a visit to the good Master, my Mother goes to bed, tired and stiff all over, but as always, concerned for others.

Translated by Mary G. Berg.

TRAVELS THROUGH THE BRAZILS

Ida Pfeiffer

Ida Pfeiffer (1797-1858) was born into a family of five broth
ers in Vienna, Austria. She was raised and treated as one of the
boys, participating in outdoor chores and activities with her
father and her brothers. Through this and the strict upbringing
of her mother, Ida developed a sense of independence and personal physical strength that would follow her throughout her
travels around the world.

At the age of nine, Ida's father died and her mother encouraged her to become more feminine by wearing dresses and taking piano lessons. Reluctantly Ida obeyed her mother. In 1820,
Ida, twenty-two years old, married Pfeiffer, a lawyer and an
Austrian government official. Soon after their marriage, her
husband lost his government position, leaving them too poor to
support themselves and their two sons. Ida's mother died in
1831, leaving Ida with a small inheritance that she put toward

the education of her sons. By 1842, Ida's sons were grown and she was divorced, leaving her free of family obligations. Taking advantage of her freedom, Ida began to travel on her own, which was often dangerous for women at this time.

Her first trip was to the Holy Land, a journey that included sailing the Danube River to the Black Sea and from there on to Constantinople, Jerusalem, Cairo, and Italy. She wrote about this journey in *Visit to the Holy Land, Egypt, and Italy,* which was published in 1846, the same year she undertook her next journey. In 1846, she ventured to Brazil, sailed around Cape Horn to Chile, and then on to Tahiti, China, The East Indies, India, Persia, Armenia, Asiatic Russia, European Russia, and Greece. Following this adventure, she wrote, *A Lady's Second Journey Around the World,* which became a best-seller. After the publication of this text, Ida was nominated into the Geographical Societies of Berlin and Paris, but the Royal Geographical Society of Great Britain refused to admit her because she was a woman. The success of this book enabled Ida to afford a trip to Iceland, where she wrote a detailed journal of her observations of Icelandic life, *Journey to Iceland, and Travels in Sweden and Norway.*

With more determination and independence than ever before, Ida continued her travels and made a trip to Madagascar, off the coast of Africa, when she came down with a tropical disease from which she never completely recovered. Ida Pfeiffer died in Vienna in 1858.

THE VOYAGE TO THE BRAZILS

6th Otober. We had at first intended to stop only one day in Novo Friburgo, and then continue our journey. Unfortunately, however, the wound which the Count had received on our excursion to Petropolis became, through the frequent use of the hand and the excessive heat, much worse; inflammation set in, and he was consequently obliged to give up all ideas of going any further. With my wounds I was more fortunate, for, as they were on the upper part of the arm, I had been enabled to pay them a proper degree of care and attention; they were now proceeding very favourably, and neither dangerous nor troublesome. I had, therefore, no resource left but either to pursue my journey alone, or to give up the most interesting portion of it, namely, my visit to the Indians. To this last idea I could by no means reconcile myself; I inquired, therefore, whether the journey could be made with any degree of safety, and as I received a sort of half-satisfactory answer, and Herr Lindenroth found me also a trusty guide, I procured a good double-barrelled pistol and set out undaunted upon my trip.

We at first remained for some time in the midst of mountain ranges, and then again descended into the warmer region beneath. The valleys were generally narrow, and the uniform appearance of the woods was often broken by plantations. The latter, however, did not always look very promising, most of them being so choked up with weeds that it was frequently impossible to perceive the plant itself, especially when it was young and small. It is only upon the sugar and coffee plantations that any great care is bestowed.

The coffee-trees stand in rows upon tolerably steep hillocks. They attain a height of from six to twelve feet, and begin to bear sometimes as soon as the second, but in no case later than the third year, and are productive for ten years. The leaf is long and slightly serrated, the blossom white, while the fruit hangs down in the same manner as a bunch of grapes, and resembles a longish cherry, which is first green, then red, brown, and nearly black. During the time it is red, the outer shell is soft, but ultimately becomes perfectly hard, and resembles a wooden capsule. Blossoms and fruit at full maturity are found upon the trees at the same time, and hence the harvest lasts nearly the whole year. The latter is conducted in two ways. The berries are either gathered by hand, or large straw mats are spread underneath, and the trees well shaken. The first method is the more troublesome, but, without comparison, the better one.

Another novelty, which I saw here for the first time, were the frequent burning forests, which had been set on fire to clear the ground for cultivation. In most cases I merely saw immense clouds of smoke curling upwards in the distance, and desired nothing more earnestly than to enjoy a nearer view of such a conflagration. My wish was destined to be fulfilled today, as my road lay between a burning forest and a burning *rost* [a strip of low brushwood that's grown up where the forest had previously been burned]. The intervening space was not, at the most, more than fifty paces broad, and was completely enveloped in smoke. I could hear the cracking of the fire, and through the dense vapour perceive thick, forked columns of flame shoot up toward the sky, while now and then loud reports, like those of a cannon, announced the fall of the large trees. On seeing my guide enter this fiery gulf, I was, I must confess, rather frightened; but I felt assured, on reflecting, that he would certainly not foolishly risk his own life, and that he must know from experience that such places were passable.

At the entrance sat two negroes, to point out the direction that wayfarers had to follow, and to recommend them to make as much haste as possible. My guide translated for me what they said, and spurred on his mule; I followed his example, and we both galloped at full speed into the smoking pass. The burning ashes now flew around us in all directions, while the suffocating smoke was even more oppressive than the heat; our beasts, too, seemed to have great difficulty in drawing breath, and it was as much as we could do to keep them in a gallop. Fortunately we had not above 500 or 600 paces to ride, and consequently suceeeded in making our way safely through.

In the Brazils a conflagration of this kind never extends very far, as the vegetation is too green and offers too much opposition. The wood has to be ignited in several places, and even then the fire frequently goes out, and when most of the wood is burnt, many patches are found unconsumed. Soon after passing this dangerous spot, we came to a magnificent rock, the sides of which must have risen almost perpendicularly to a height of 600 or 800 feet. A number of detached fragments lay scattered about the road, forming picturesque groups.

To my great astonishment, I learned from my guide that our lodging for the night was near at hand; we had scarcely ridden twenty miles, but he affirmed that the next *venda* where we could stop was too far distant. I afterwards discovered that his sole object was to spin out the journey, which was a very profitable one for him, since, besides good living for himself, and fodder for his two mules, he received four milreis *(8s.8d.)* a day. We put up, therefore, at a solitary venda, erected in the middle of the forest, and kept by Herr Molasz.

During the day we had suffered greatly from the heat; the thermometer standing, in the sun, at 119° 75' Fah.

The circumstance which must strike a traveller most forcibly in the habits of the colonists and inhabitants of the Brazils is the contrast between fear and courage. On the one hand, every one you meet upon the road is armed with pistols and long knives, as if the whole country were overrun with robbers and murderers, while, on the other, the proprietors live quite alone on their plantations, and without the least apprehension, in the midst of their numerous slaves. The traveller, too, fearlessly passes the night in some *venda*, situated in impenetrable woods, with neither shutters to the windows nor good locks to the doors, besides which the owner's room is a considerable distance from the chambers of the guests, and it would be utterly impossible to obtain any assistance from the servants, who are all slaves, as they live either in some corner of the stable, or in the loft. At first I felt very frightened at this passing the night alone, surrounded by the wild gloom of the forest, and in a room that was only very insecurely fastened; but, as I was everywhere assured that such a thing as a forcible entry into a house had never been heard of, I soon dismissed my superfluous anxiety, and enjoyed the most tranquil repose.

I know very few countries in Europe where I should like to traverse vast forests, and pass the night in such awfully lonely houses, accompanied by only a hired guide.

On the 7th of October, also, we made only a short day's journey of twenty miles, to the small town of Canto Gallo. The scenery was of the usual description, consisting of narrow, circumscribed valleys and mountains covered with endless forests. If little *fazendas*, and the remains of woods which had been set on fire, had not, every now and then, reminded us of the hand of man, I should have thought that I was wandering through some yet undiscovered part of Brazil.

The monotony of our journey was rather romantically interrupted by our straying for a short distance from the right road. In order to reach it again, we were obliged to penetrate, by untrodden paths, through the woods; a task presenting difficulties of which a European can scarcely form an idea. We dismounted from our mules, and my guide threw back, on either side, the low-hanging branches, and cut through the thick web of creepers; while, one moment, we were obliged to climb over broken trunks, or squeeze ourselves between others, at the next we sank knee-deep among endless parasitioal plants. I began almost to despair of ever effecting a passage, and, even up to the present day, am at a loss to understand how we suceeeded in escaping from this inextricable mass.

The little town of Canto Gallo is situated in a narrow valley, and contains about eighty houses. The *venda* stands apart, the town not being visible from it. The temperature here is warm as in Rio de Janeiro.

On my return to the *venda*, after a short walk to the town, I applied to my landlady, in order to obtain a near and really correct idea of a Brazilian household. The good woman, however, gave herself very little trouble, either in looking after the house or the kitchen; as is the case in Italy, this was her husband's business. A negress and two young negroes cooked, the arrangements of the kitchen being of the most primitive simplicity. The salt was pressed fine with a bottle; the potatoes, when boiled, underwent the same process—the latter were also subsequently squeezed in the frying pan with a plate, to give them the form of a pancake; a pointed piece of wood served for a fork, &c. There was a large fire burning for every dish.

Every one whose complexion was white, sat down with us at table. All the dishes, consisting of cold roast beef, black beans with boiled *carna secca* [long strips of beef which have been salted and dried], potatoes, rice, manioc flour, and boiled manioc root, were placed upon the table at the same time, and every one helped himself as he pleased. At the conclusion of our meal, we had strong coffee without milk. The slaves had beans, carna secca, and manioc flour.

8th October. Our goal today was the *Fazenda* Boa Esperanza, twenty-four miles off. Four miles beyond Canto Gallo, we crossed a small waterfall, and then entered one of the most magnificent virgin forests I had yet beheld. A small path, on the bank of a little brook conducted us through it. Palms, with their majestic tops, raised themselves proudly above the other trees, which, lovingly interlaced together, formed the most beautiful bowers; orchids grew in wanton luxurience upon the branches and twigs; creepers and ferns climbed up the trees, mingling with the boughs, and forming thick walls of blossoms and flowers, which displayed the most brilliant colours, and exhaled the sweetest perfume; delicate hummingbirds twittered around our heads; the pepper-peeker, with his brilliant plumage, soared shily upwards; parrots and parroquets were swinging themselves in the branches, and numberless beautifully marked birds, which I only knew from having seen specimens in the Museum, inhabited this fairy grove. It seemed as if I was riding in some fairy park, and I expected, every moment, to see sylphs and nymphs appear before me.

I was so happy, that I felt richly recompensed for all the fatigue of my journey. One thought only obscured this beautiful picture; and that was that weak man should dare to enter the lists with the giant nature of the place, and make it bend before his will. How soon, perhaps, may this profound and holy tranquillity be disturbed by the blows of some daring settler's axe, to make room for the wants of men!

I saw no dangerous animals save a few dark green snakes, from five to seven feet long; a dead ounce, that had been stripped of its skin; and a lizard, three feet in length, which ran timidly across our path. I met with no apes; they appear to conceal themselves deeper in the woods, where no human footstep is likely to disturb them in their sports and gambols.

During the whole distance from Canto Gallo to the small village of St. Ritta (sixteen miles), if it had not again been for a few coffee plantations, I should have thought the place completely forgotten by man.

Near St. Ritta are some gold-washings in the river of the same name, and not far from them, diamonds also are found. Since seeking or digging for diamonds is no longer an imperial monopoly, every one is at liberty to employ himself in this occupation, and yet it is exercised as much as possible in secret. No one will acknowledge looking for them, in order to avoid paying the State its share as fixed by law. The precious stones are sought for and dug out at certain spots, from heaps of sand, stones, and soil, which have been washed down by the heavy rains.

I had found lodgings in a *venda* for the last time, the preceding evening, at Canto Gallo. I had now to rely upon the hospitality of the proprietors of the *fazendas*. Custom requires that, on reaching a *fazenda*, any person who desires to stop the middle of the day or the night there, should wait outside and ask, through the servant, permission to do so. It is not until his application is granted, which is almost always the case, that the traveller dismounts from his mule, and enters the building.

They received me at the *Fazenda* of Boa Esperanza in the most friendly manner, and, as I happened to arrive exactly at dinner-time (it was between 3 and 4 o'clock), covers were immediately laid for me and my attendant. The dishes were numerous, and prepared very nearly in the European fashion.

Great astonishment was manifested in every *venda* and *fazenda* at seeing a lady arrive accompanied only by a single servant. The first question was whether I was not afraid thus to traverse the woods alone, and my guide was invariably taken on one side, and questioned as to why I travelled. As he was in the habit of seeing me collect flowers and insects, he supposed me to be a naturalist, and replied that my journey had a scientific object.

After dinner, the amiable lady of the house proposed that I should go and see the coffee plantations, warehouses, &c. and I willingly accepted her offer, as affording me an opportunity of viewing the manner in which the coffee was prepared, from beginning to end.

The mode of gathering it I have already described. When this is done, the coffee is spread out upon large plots of ground, trodden down in a peculiar manner, and enclosed by low stone walls, scarcely a foot high, with little drain-holes in them, to allow of the water running off in case of rain. On these places the coffee is dried by the glowing heat of the sun, and then shaken in large stone mortars, ten or twenty of which are placed beneath a wooden scaffolding, from which wooden hammers, set in motion by water power, descend into the mortars, and easily crush the husks. The mass, thus crushed, is then placed in wooden boxes, fastened in the middle of a long table, and having small openings at each side, through which both the berry itself and the husk fall slowly out. At the table are seated negroes, who separate the berry from the husk, and then cast it into shallow copper cauldrons, which are easily heated. In these it is carefully turned, and remains until it is quite dried. This last process requires some degree of care, as the colour of the coffee depends upon the degree of heat to which it is exposed; if dried too quickly, instead of the usual greenish colour, it contracts a yellowish tinge.

On the whole, the preparation of coffee is not fatiguing, and even the gathering of it is far from being as laborious as reaping is with us. The negro stands in an upright posture when gathering the berry, and is protected by the tree itself against the great heat of the sun. Tho only danger he incurs is of being bitten by some venomous snake or other—an accident, however, which, fortunately, rarely happens.

The work on a sugar-plantation, on the contrary, is said to be exceedingly laborious, particularly that portion of it which relates to weeding the ground and cutting the cane. I have never yet witnessed a sugar-harvest, but, perhaps, may do so in the course of my travels.

All work ceases at sunset, when the negroes are drawn up in front of their master's house for the purpose of being counted, and then, after a short prayer, have their supper, consisting of boiled beans, bacon, carna secca, and manioc flour, handed out to them. At sunrise, they again assemble, are once more counted, and, after prayers and breakfast, go to work.

I had an opportunity of convincing myself in this, as well as in many other *fazendas, vendas,* and private houses, that the slaves are by far not so harshly treated as we Europeans imagine. They are not overworked, perform all their duties very leisurely, and are well kept. Their children are frequently the playmates of their master's children, and knock each other about as if they were all equal. There may be cases in which certain slaves are cruelly and undeservedly punished; but do not the like instances of injustice occur in Europe also?

I am certainly very much opposed to slavery, and should greet its abolition with the greatest delight, but, despite this, I again affirm that the negro slave enjoys, under the protection of the law, a better lot than the free *fellah* of Egypt, or many peasants in Europe, who still groan under the right of socage. The principal reason of the better lot of the slave, compared to that of the miserable peasant, in the case in point, may perhaps partly be, that the purchase and keep of the one is expensive, while the other costs nothing.

The arrangements in the houses belonging to the proprietors of the *fazendas* are extremely simple. The windows are unglazed, and are closed at night with wooden shutters. In many instances, the outer roof is the common covering of all the rooms, which are merely separated from one another by low partitions, so that you ean hear every word your neighbour says, and almost the breathing of the person sleeping next to you. The furniture is equally simple: a large table, a few straw sofas, and a few chairs. The wearing apparel is generally hung up against the walls; the linen alone being kept in tin cases, to protect it from the attacks of the ants.

In the country, the children of even the most opulent persons run about frequently without shoes or stockings. Before they go to bed they have their feet examined to see whether any sand-fleas have nestled in them; and if such be the case, they are extracted by the elder negro children.

9th October. Early in the morning I took leave of my kind hostess, who, like a truly careful housewife, had wrapped up a roasted fowl, manioc flour, and a cheese for me, so that I was well provisioned on setting off.

The next station, Aldea do Pedro, on the banks of the Parahyby, was situated at a distance of sixteen miles. Our way lay through magnificent woods, and before we had traversed half of it, we arrived at the river Parahyby, one of the largest in the Brazils, and celebrated, moreover, for the peculiar character of its bed, which is strewed with innumerable cliffs and rocks; these, owing to the low state of the stream, were more than usually conspicuous. On every side rose little islands, covered with small trees or underwood, lending a most magic appearance to the river. During the rainy season, most of these cliffs and rocks are covered with water, and the river then appears more majestic. On account of the rocks it can only be navigated by small boats and rafts.

As you proceed along the banks, the greenery gradually changes. The fore-part of the mountain ranges subside into low hills, the mountains themselves retreat, and the nearer you approach Aldea do Pedro, the wider and more open becomes the valley. In the background alone are still visible splendid mountain ranges, from which rises a mountain higher than the rest, somewhat more naked, and almost isolated. To this my guide pointed, and gave me to understand that our way lay over it, in order to reach the Puris, who lived beyond.

About noon I arrived at Aldea do Pedro, which I found to be a small village with a stone church; the latter might, perhaps, contain 200 persons. I had intended continuing my journey to the Puris the same day, but my guide was attacked with pains in his knee, and could not ride further. I had, therefore, no resource but to alight at the priest's, who gave me a hearty welcome; he had a pretty good house, immediately adjoining the church.

10th October. As my guide was worse, the priest offered me his negro to replace him. I thankfully accepted his offer, but could not set off before one o'clock, for which I was, in some respects, not sorry, as it was Sunday, and I hoped to see a great number of the country people flock to mass. This, however, was not the case; although it was a very fine day there were hardly thirty people at church. The men were dressed exactly in the European fashion; the women wore long cloaks with collars, and had white handkerchiefs upon their heads, partly falling over their faces as well; the latter they uncovered in church. Both men and women were barefooted.

As chance would have it, I witnessed a burial and a christening. Before mass commenced, a boat crossed over from the opposite bank of the Parahyby, and on reaching the side, a hammock, in which was the deceased, was lifted out. He was then laid in a coffin which had been prepared for the purpose in a house near the churchyard. The corpse was enveloped in a white cloth, with the feet and half the head protruding beyond it; the latter was covered with a peaked cap of shining black cloth.

The christening took place before the burial. The person who was to be christened was a young negro of fifteen, who stood with his mother at the church door. As the priest entered the church to perform mass, he christened him, in passing by, without much ceremony or solemnity, and even without sponsors; the boy, too, seemed to be as little touched by the whole affair as a newborn infant. I do not believe that either he or his mother had the least idea of the importance of the rite.

The priest then hurriedly performed mass, and read the burial service over the deceased, who had belonged to rather a wealthy family, and therefore was respectably interred. Unfortunately, when they wanted to lower the corpse into its cold resting-place, the latter was found to be too short and too narrow, and the poor wretch was so tossed about, coffin and all, that I expected every moment to see him roll out. But all was of no avail, and after a great deal of useless exertion no other course was left but to place the coffin on one side and enlarge the grave, which was done with much unwillingness and amid an unceasing volley of oaths.

This fatiguing work being at last finished, I returned to the house, where I took a good *déjeuner á la fourchette* in company with the priest, and then set out with my black guide.

We rode for some time through a broad valley between splendid woods, and had to cross two rivers, the Parahyby and the Pomba, in trunks of trees hollowed out. For each of these wretched conveyances I was obliged to pay one milreis *(2s.2d.)*, and to incur great danger into the bargain; not so much on account of the stream and the small size of the craft, as of our mules, which, fastened by their halter, swam alongside, and frequently came so near that I was afraid that we should be every moment capsized.

After riding twelve miles further, we reached the last settlement of the whites. On an open space, which had with difficulty been conquered from the virgin forest, stood a largish wooden house surrounded by a few miserable huts, the house serving as the residence of the whites, and the huts as that of the slaves. A letter which I had brought from the priest procured me a welcome.

The manner of living in this settlement was of such a description that I was almost tempted to believe that I was already among savages.

The large house contained an entrance hall lending into four rooms, each of which was inhabited by a white family. The whole furniture of these rooms consisted of a few hammocks and straw mats. The inhabitants were cowering upon the floor, playing with the children, or assisting one another to get rid of their vermin. The kitchen was immediately adjoining the house, and resembled a very large barn with openings in it; upon a hearth that took up nearly the entire length of the barn, several fires were burning, over which hung small kettles, and at each side were fastened wooden spits. On these were fixed several pieces of meat, some of which were being roasted by the fire and some cured by the smoke. The kitchen was full of people: whites, Puris, and negroes, children whose parents were whites and Puris, or Puris and negroes—in a word, the place was like a book of specimens containing the most varied ramifications of the three principal races of the country.

* * *

I passed the night, therefore, with these half savages, who constantly showed me the greatest respect, and overwhelmed me with attention. A straw mat, which, at my request, was spread out under shelter in the courtyard, was my bed. They brought me for supper a roast fowl, rice, and hard eggs, and for dessert, oranges and tamarind-pods; the latter contain a brown, half-sweet, half-sour pulp very agreeable to the taste. The women lay all round me, and by degrees we managed to get on wonderfully together.

Translated by William Hazlet.

TRAVELS THROUGH
CENTRAL AMERICA & MEXICO

Helen Sanborn

Helen Josephine Sanborn (1857-1927) was born in Greene, Maine. Her father, James Sanborn, was a leader in the distribution of imported spices and coffee. Guatemala had become a center for the haarvesting of coffee beans. After Helen's graduation from Wellesley College in the spring of 1884, she accompanied her father on an expedition from Boston to Guatemala, having offered to learn Spanish so that she could join her father as his intrpreter. An avid traveler with her Wellesley classmates, Helen became an ambassador of the Hispanic cultures in her support of Spanish language and cultural studies at academic institutions. Helen was a leader in the establishment of Instituto Internacional in Madrid, an institute for North

American young women to learn Spanish, which is still active today. She died at the age of seventy after a protracted illness. Her book, *A Winter in Central America*, documents the challenges and marvels that Helen Sanborn experienced as she traveled by train, boat, mule, and foot to Guatemala.

CHARACTER AND CUSTOMS OF THE PEOPLE

The population of Guatemala is given as one million four hundred thousand, but the census is not very exact, and probably there are a million and a half of people. Of these nearly a million 50,000 are Indians, three hundred thousand *ladinos*, and about one hundred and eighty thousand whites, including Spaniards and foreigners.

The characteristics of the Indians have already been described, but we wish to add something about their origin. There are twenty different tribes, each with its own language; but all save three or four belong to the same family the general name of the Indians of Guatemala being that of "Quiche."

They trace their origin through a long line of kings back to the ancient Toltecs, who formerly inhabited Mexico, the majority of whom were driven out by the coming of the Aztec in the eleventh century. These Toltecs are supposed to have been the most superior race of Indians that ever inhabited this continent. They possessed a wonderful civilization, and all the finest architectural remains and ruins in the country (those of Yucatan and some parts of Mexico) are attributed to this race. When the Aztecs came, the Toltecs, not being a warlike people, offered no resistance, but some of them moved further south, while a part remained, became amalgamated with the Aztecs, and taught them their wonderful civilization—that civilization which so astonished Cortez and his army when they entered Mexico, and remains of which are still to be seen in the city at this day. Unlike the Aztecs, their history is not stained by the offerings of human sacrifice on the altars of their gods, nor by the horrible practice of cannibalism. To the traveller it is most interesting to note how the present Indian tribes and the other inhabitants of Guatemala differ from those of Mexico. But of this we shall speak later on. Morelet, the naturalist, who has given greatest study to these "Quiche" Indians, describes them as "an active, courageous race, whose heads never grow gray, persevering in their industry, skillful in almost every department of art, good workers in iron and the precious metals, generally well dressed, neat in person, with a firm step and independent bearing, and altogether constituting a class of citizens who only require to be better educated to rise equal to the best."

Their condition has already been shown. It seemed to us, as near as we could determine, very much like that of the serfs in the old feudal system. We were told that if a man bought a piece of ground, the Indians on that land were bound to work for him. Roads are built and repaired, aqueducts made, and the government coffee plantations all carried on by "forced labor," the poor Indians working without a cent of pay. As we have shown, they do the hardest work for the smallest pay, and have but few rights. They have the power to choose, subject to the approval of the *Jefe*, one of their number as *alcalde*, a sort of judge, to whom they appeal for protection and justice. This is their only voice in the government.

The *ladinos*, especially the lower class, are inferior to the Indians in cleanliness, honesty, and industry. Still, they regard themselves as infinitely superior, and treat the Indians with great contempt.

The dress of the people is characteristic. That of the Indians has been described. In and about the capital it is somewhat different from that of the interior, in that the women, instead of wearing a loose skirt, take a straight piece of cloth and wind it tightly about them, with an awkward effect. One tribe near Antigua dresses in black. The women of the lower class wear an embroidered chemise, a full skirt, and a bright colored *rebosa* (a single shawl), over the shoulders and head, as they never wear hats. Of the higher classes, the wealthiest have adopted the European dress; and often the costumes are imported from Paris, and are very elegant. Very few use hats, but they wear very gracefully the Spanish *mantilla* upon their heads, and the black shawl of fine texture over the shoulders. It is said that "when the ladies put on hats they leave off smoking." These varied costumes, so different from ours, make the streets a gay and novel scene to the traveller.

All the people, whether of Spanish or mixed blood, are truly Spanish in their customs and manner of life. Boys and girls are placed in separate schools, even in their youngest years, and girls are most carefully watched and secluded. The streets are full of Indian women, but one sees very few of the higher classes, and this was so noticeable that we asked, "Where are the ladies of Guatemala?" and received the answer, "In their houses." It is contrary to custom and all rules of etiquette for a lady to go on the street alone, even in the daytime. She must be attended by a servant or another companion, and it is improper for ladies, even in groups of two or three, to be out after dark unattended by a servant. Ladies and gentlemen never walk together on the street unless married.

An American girl does not half appreciate her freedom and independence until she goes to one of these countries. Indeed, the American and German ladies have found these customs so tiresome and disagreeable that they have rather broken over them, and now if a stranger walks the street unattended she is forgiven by the people, who have learned that the customs of other nations are different from their own.

The young ladies being kept so secluded by the Spanish custom, love-making must necessarily conform to circumstances; and the suitor, since he is not allowed admission into the presence of his *inamorata*, frequents the pavement in front of her house, and gazes up at her balcony, where she sits ensconced behind the bars. This performance is called in Mexico *hacer el oso* (playing the bear), and in Spain *pelando la pava* (plucking the turkey). It is often continued for months, and even years, without success, the result depending upon the will of the parents, who, after a time, make inquiries into the young man's prospects, and, if the results are satisfactory, invite him into the house, although they never allow him to see the young lady alone.

Naturally, the young peope make the most of every meeting at the theatre, opera, and Plaza, where, by motions and glances, they carry on most extensive and ridiculous "flirtations." The Mexicans especially, as every traveller will observe, indulge in this folly to the greatest degree.

Spanish gentlemen consider it complimentary to stare at a lady, and will even put their heads into a carriage where one is sitting, and gaze at her steadily for several minutes. American ladies of blond complexion travelling in these countries get so much admiration of this nature that it is exceedingly disagreeable, and even painful. Blue eyes and light hair are so rare that they are greatly admired, and boys will often stand and look up into a lady's face for some time, and pour forth a constant stream of compliments, which, if she understands Spanish, is truly overpowering.

These customs strike an American as very peculiar, and make him exclaim, "Consistency, thou art a jewel," for there is a great show of virtue and little of the reality. The whole Spanish system of society gives plainest evidence of its falsity, and the fact that it defeats its own purpose. The words of Lara, in "The Spanish Student," regarding the lack of virtue among Spanish women, are often repeated in Guatemala and Mexico.

That the moral state of society is low, there can be no doubt. Most deplorable of all is the existence of evils similar to those in the South during the time of slavery. That the Indian women are not lacking in virtue, however, is proved by the fact that many beautiful Indian maidens appeal to their *Jefe* for the protection of the law against the wealthy planters.

Gambling and drinking, especially the former, are carried to excess. We saw much less drunkenness in all the time we were away than can be seen in one week in the city of Boston. But gambling exists to an alarming extent, although no more among the natives than among the foreign population. Poker is the favorite game; playing cards without money is never thought of; whist parties, composed of both ladies and gentlemen, meet regularly Sunday nights to play *con dinero* (for money).

In Guatemala, as in all these countries, Sunday is the great holiday. The market is then most crowded; the stores most largely patronized; the best plays are presented at the Opera; and the bull fight occurs. There are very few, even among the Americans, who observe the Sabbath after they have been there a while.

It is surprising how soon Germans and Americans fall into the ways of the country, giving as their excuse a phrase we heard until we were heartily disgusted, *Hay la costumbre en Centro America* (It is the custom in Central America.), as if with a change of climate it were necessary to change one's sense of propriety, and even one's ideas of right and wrong.

The prevalence of smoking has been alluded to. It sounds rather peculiar, but is no uncommon question to ask a lady if she smokes, and many foreign ladies, both young and old, adopt the practice, although we are happy to say we saw no American ladies who smoked.

One of the most hopeless features in regard to the state of society there is this lack of a sense of responsibility on the part of foreigners, both Americans and Germans. They are a superior race, who have had better advantages, and are so looked upon by the people; but instead of doing anything to elevate the country, the majority of them simply adopt its vices and then condemn the people for the same sins.

Our personal experience with the people was so pleasant that we dislike to think at all of their faults. We met many truly good people, whose kindness impressed us more than the wickedness of the greater number, and makes us feel well disposed toward the whole. Travel across the country as we did, and partake of their hospitality, and remember their origin and history, and you will love them in spite of their wickedness. But if you want to be convinced of the doctrine of total depravity, get some of the foreign residents of Guatemala to talking about the natives. They will grant them no excellences whatever. They will tell you the people are false, deceitful, treacherous, and desperately wicked; that they are polite and say kind things without meaning a word of it, simply to flatter you and make you pleased with yourself and them; and that they never do a kindness save from a selfish motive. We could not believe this, and on mentioning one and another, even all of the natives with whom we had any dealings, we were always assured that these were indeed most excellent and thoroughly good men. Was it, then, that we met only exceptions? If so, we are glad, and we know at least here were some as good and true as live in any part of the world.

Two characteristics of the people (most trying to all who deal with them) are certainly to be condemned. These are their indolence and dilatoriness. They are slow and lazy, as a rule, and will never do to-day what can be put off until tomorrow. They lack the energy and enterprise so characteristic of Americans. But then, again, we could well learn from them both patience and amiability. They did seem the most patient, amiable people in the world. We never saw a person among them in an ill humor, never heard any cross words, or witnessed a single quarrel. Americans might learn much, too, from this simple, warm-hearted people in politeness, courtesy, and hospitality, for as compared with them we are cold, stiff, formal, and selfish.

They have many little expressions of salutation and leave-taking, and forms of compliment, which have no equivalents in English, but which are very pretty and very pleasing to the traveller who knows a little of the language. You can but feel more kindly disposed toward the bright, black-eyed young fellow who takes care of your room, when he greets you every morning in the pleasant way with *buenos dias*, and on bringing you your candle at night says, *duerme bien* (sleep well), or *pasa buena noche*; and you cannot feel half as irritated over a poor bargain at one of the stores when the clerk politely bows you out with an "adios."

If Spanish politeness is false and hollow we did not find it out. If kind words were said without meaning, simply to make us pleased with the speaker, the result was surely accomplished, and we felt more kindly disposed toward the whole of Guatemala for the pleasant words spoken in that musical language. Many acts of real kindness and self-sacrifice we know were extended us from the pure good will of the people; if any were done from a selfish motive, it is no more than we meet with every day at home. From our personal experience with the people from first to last, we can but speak with affection and gratitude of all.

TRAVELS THROUGH NICARAGUA

Dora Hort

Navigating verdant landscapes, azure rivers, and unknown people, Dora Hort traveled by boat from New York to San Francisco in the first half of the 1880s. In 1887, she published her travel memoir, *Via Nicaragua*, where Hort documents her voyage through the Nicaraguan isthmus. Her sister, four nieces and nephews, a male servant, gentleman companion, and New York society lifestyle accompanied Hort on her first sojourn through the Central American landscapes. Writing in her own voice, Dora Hort shows her bewildered enamorment for the animals and people that occupied the majestic ecology and the food and music these lands bore.

THE LAND TRANSIT

The fact of there being no beaten track, no road by which to be guided, were startling facts that soon dawned upon us. As we could perceive nothing that at all resembled a path, we were constantly obliged to retrace our steps, having arrived at points from which there was no possible outlet. These incessant obstacles were not only aggravating, but they very considerably increased my consternation respecting my sister's absence, as in the fashion we were proceeding the chances of her overtaking us became less and less probable.

The route was through a vast labyrinth of dense forest, so sombre and silent that it awed one; and I began to suspect from seeing no trace of any other passenger that we had strayed in a wrong direction.

I likewise fancied that M. Pioche shared my apprehension, for he stopped the first native we saw and engaged him to guide us. This man produced a long knife, and at once commenced to cut away the bush seaward, a point he knew, happily for us, as there was no regular road. Occasionally we caught glimpses of grand scenery and paused to admire it, when the stupid guide, regardless of our so doing, would march on and leave us to find our way as best we could. The path he made in advance of us soon became imperceptible unless passed over while the guide was still in sight. The result was that the imbecile had to be hallooed back to our assistance, and by this time the finest scenery in the world would have failed to impress me, so great was my dismay. These frequent recalls occasioned much unnecessary detention, and retarded our progress to a serious degree; naturally we were all exceedingly anxious to reach our destination before dark, and it began to look doubtful. It was, however, a grand old forest through which we were with so much difficulty endeavouring to make our way over masses of trailing foliage. The prolific parasites were entwined round the majestic trees, and drooped in graceful tendrils between branches; from decayed barks hung clusters of bright-hued blossoms, orchids no doubt, though I did not know them as such, my horticultural knowledge about the higher order of lichens being then very imperfect.

Brilliantly plumed birds twittered and fluttered overhead, startled into unusual activity by our unexpected approach. The gloomy solitude and grandeur of the scene became each moment more intensified, as precipitous ascents, with the probable descents on the other side, loomed before our eyes. We had gradually quitted the bush and luxuriant foliage to arrive at a far bolder description of scenery, when hills and deep glens intersected by waterfalls were charming to look at, but rugged to clamber over; however, so long as the animal I rode played no tricks to unseat me, and I was able to keep my extremely uncomfortable position on the Mexican saddle, I was quite prepared to endure, as well as admire the magnificent scene that surrounded us.

Some of these perpendicular eminences were thickly wooded, and sloped down to gloomy ravines over which we had to pick our steps with the greatest caution. I confess that with all my boasted courage, it was with a faint heart and trembling frame that I traversed such wild, weird defiles, spots which probably had never before been trodden by human feet, or the silence disturbed by the sound of profane language as was then the case! Fortunately for my nerves, the mule I rode was tractable, and condescended to steer clear of branches that threatened my face, and avoided passing close to the trunks of trees to the injury of my limbs; such pranks being the usual practice of the Nicaragua Isthmus donkeys and mules, whether with the object of unseating the rider, or the express purpose of doing him a cruel injury, it is difficult to determine.

Joseph Pioche rode one of those vicious brutes which persistently grazed his legs against the gnarled trunks, and damaged his face with the low-lying branches, nor did all the abusive epithets, blows, and savage kicks make the slightest impression; indeed, these attempts at coercion were invariably resented by a roll on the grass, when the antics of both man and beast were truly ludicrous. The action of the latter seemed to imply that, finding jamming, bruising, and scratching could not rid him of his rider, a roll would. And such was positively the case. Joseph clung on to his back, determined to brave all rather than be mastered, though at the same time he looked capable of killing the animal, even if by so doing he should be obliged to trudge the rest of the route on foot. He was on each occasion persuaded to remount by his cousin; the "Courage, *mon ami*," had the effect of raising all the pluck at his command; combined with this was the desire to prove to us that he did not lack moral or physical stamina.

We unanimously advised the poor fellow not to jerk at the reins, to leave them loose, as his savage tugs might tend to exasperate the animal, and render him the more stubborn. As the trees became wider apart, we appeared in a fair way to have no further annoyance in that quarter, and were enabled to resume our ride. For a short space this quietude lasted, when suddenly the air resounded with a furious yell, which caused a general halt. We looked back with craned necks, and descried Joseph actually hanging from a branch of a tree, not like Absalom by the hair, as he was bald, but by his hands, which he had outstretched in time to save himself, while the mule passed on, freed of his rider, who remained suspended in mid-air. Thus this most mulish of mules had persevered, and come off victorious. Furious blows and kicks were bestowed on him before he received the order to get out of the way, which he for the first time obeyed, with such alacrity, indeed that it was greeted with a burst of laughter.

Another animal of the same breed was obtained from a native who had joined us, and we resumed our route, but this time mirthless, as the constant halts and delays had been a great drawback to speed, while, from what the guide said, the most dangerous passages were yet to be traversed.

We had already crossed numbers of torrents, some of them were swollen to the size of rivers, yet these also we had to ford, and as we descended a mountain we approached one that was still more formidable, at the sight of which I was so terrified that it must have been reflected on my face. Fortunately at this point we, for the first time, fell in with a large number of our fellow-passengers; here we drew rein, and watched their struggling efforts to reach the opposite side, flanked by a steep slippery rock, to be climbed before a safe footing could be obtained.

Not the smallest particle of soil was discernible between the torrent and the base of this hideous declivity. As the water quite reached to the body of the animals, no one escaped a wetting. I shuddered at the idea of this description of foot-bath, and shrank from the prospect, when help, unlooked-for help, came to me through the person of one of our second-cabin passengers—a tall, powerful Yorkshireman, who was equipped in long, heavy boots, the tops of which reached his waist. His pretty, delicate wife was on a mule with her baby, while he carried in his arms his little son.

Coming up to my side, he said, "Have nought to fear; yonder on the ship ye spake kindly to my lass and bairn; when I have taken them over I will return and do the same for ye." And so he did. Cautioning me to hold up my skirts and feet as high as

I could, he led my mule over, and mounted the steep rock, never slackening his grasp of the rope until he left me on a level spot where I felt once more safe.

I was, as may be imagined, eloquent in my acknowledgment to this handsome, surly giant, who had hitherto never vouchsafed me even a recognition. Truly does a soft word turn away wrath, as I knew of nothing else for which he or his had been beholden to me!

On the other side of the torrent was a grand spectacle of mountains, rocks, cascades, and roaring torrents. Save for the music of falling water, or a fragment of rock becoming detached and thundering down into the ravines hundreds of feet below, the silence was unbroken, and when I glanced down those fearful passes I shivered at the awful fate in case of a false step. Thank heaven no accident did occur!

Leaving these stupendous works of nature, we issued from their intricacies on to a wide plateau covered with soft moist turf; vines wandered and entwined their slender tendrils round the gnarled trunks and branches of trees; by this means a sort of verdant lattice was formed, which our profane hands had to tear asunder! We also frequently saw shreds of garments attached to thorny bushes; these satisfied us that others besides ourselves had passed that way. This was a great consolation to me, for I began to quake at the probable reception in store for me on meeting my deserted sister.

STARTLING INCIDENTS

Over-fatigue sometimes precludes sleep, and this was my case; I was far too tired to enjoy any repose, but not to feel a sudden and sharp pain in my ear, as if some horrid insect had stung me. I could distinguish nothing, but wondered whether I had not been bitten by a venomous snake, and by daylight might be dead and swollen past recognition! A doleful reflection certainly, but one I had to endure along with the burning sensation in my ear until dawn, when I roused my sister and asked her to examine the painful spot. She said I had been attacked by a jigger, an insect which burrows under the skin, and there deposits her eggs; neither could it be extricated without the medium of a fine needle, none of which had we at hand. She furthermore went on to explain that the greatest precaution was necessary to remove the nest intact, otherwise disagreeable consequences might ensue, which I concluded to mean a separation of the eggs and a swarm of jiggers infesting my poor ear—anything but a reassuring piece of information. It revolted me beyond measure to think that my ear had been converted into an incubator! And I decided that I had had enough of that mattress and pillow for one night, as from them I felt sure the mischief had arisen.

I looked about the crowded room in search of water to remove the previous day's accumulation of dust, but seemingly washstands were not considered at all essential in that hotel, as nothing of the sort existed; neither could I find a servant of any description whatever to supply my needs. Outside I espied Jones standing still, with his straw hat resting on the back of his head, staring seaward. His attitude and expression could not have been more despondent. In a dismal tone he called my attention to the steamer on which we were to embark for the Golden City. He said she could never accommodate our number of passengers; it could only hold a hundred at the outside, and we amounted to three times that number. Jones concluded his remarks with, "Shure the half on us will be dead before we arrive." He likewise called the Company a dirty pack of cowardly liars and thieves. It was strong language, yet I cannot say unmerited, as I entirely concurred in his opinion. Was my inflamed ear not due to the filthy floor and filthier pillow? I horrified our good Jones with a description of what had befallen me, and the fearful operation I was to undergo later in the day, with the prospect of mortification and amputation staring me in the face; festering wounds I could well conceive to be very serious matters in such a hot climate.

"Well, well, I niver," said Jones; "shure an' its actionable." But I had my doubts!

It turned out that the water in the neighbourhood of the hotel was brackish, but that there was a fresh spring some little distance off, and Jones volunteered to fetch me from thence a pitcherful which had to suffice for the family use.

As the breakfast was likely to be a repetition of the previous night's supper, we went elsewhere to seek ours. With this intention we strolled down the baked sandy beach, and met many others on the same quest.

San Juan del Sud looked what it was, an uninteresting, desolate hamlet, with a poverty stricken population, who herded in dilapidated huts, exposed to the sun and wind, as the trees that grew there afforded no shade whatsoever, being both stunted and blighted. The reason I could not explain, as the wind was warm enough and the moisture sufficient to nourish such as we saw. Certainly San Juan del Norte looked as tropical and inviting as this place appeared arid and uninviting.

Scattered down the beach were a few taverns, but neither cafe nor restaurant was anywhere visible. We entered a wooden building which presented rather a better aspect than the others. The interior had no partitions; it was a square room with a long, rough table in the centre. The inevitable bar stood at one end, and on the counter were a few bottles and glasses; at the opposite extremity a man lay stretched at full length on a wooden bench who looked a living skeleton. We took him to be in a dying condition, as a deep purple hue surrounded his sunken eyes and bloodless lips, and immediately turned to beat a precipitate retreat from such a ghastly sight, when, to our astonishment, he called out in a much stronger voice than his pitiable state warranted, to inquire what we wished. We explained that we had come in the hope of procuring breakfast for our party, which by this time had swelled into a considerable company. He replied, "I guess you can get it here if you be willin' to cook the victuals for yourselves; the eggs and bread you'll find in a drawer over there, and a plenty of ducks and fowls in the back yard."

He went on to inform us that he was down with ague—a fresh attack was on him then, and would prevent his affording us personal assistance. Some discussion then ensued among the womankind as to who were willing and capable of undertaking the culinary part of the business. When this essential question was settled the men started off in search of the poultry, while an old white man, who was loitering about the premises, was engaged to collect wood and make a fire. And in less time than it seemed practicable we sat down to what we had come to consider a sumptuous repast, composed of two immense dishes of fricasseed fowls and ducks, a large supply of fried and boiled eggs with the addition of cooked plantains; this was sufficient to satisfy thirty ravenous stomachs.

The meal was barely terminated when we were summoned to prepare for embarkation. Not till the last moment did our sick host make any attempt to move; but as we rose from table so did he from his bench, and contrived to shuffle to the back of his counter to receive payment in orthodox style. He demanded five dollars apiece, which amounted to no less a sum than one hundred and fifty dollars (thirty pounds). The money was collected, but not without a dissenting murmur by the Western members of the crowd at the extortionate charge. One woman, indeed, named Latimer, pushed her way to the front and exclaimed, "You have got your money for the victuals we ate; I now expect my pay for cooking 'em along with this here," indicating my blushing, shrinking sister. The man never dreamed of disputing her claim of five dollars apiece, exactly what she had paid for her own meal, and coolly repocketed. The obliging old party who had done all the hard work received my sister's remuneration, which he well merited; the sum was considerable, and his thanks in proportion.

My ear was troubling me both mentally and physically, and as soon as we were on board the steamer, where we could procure a needle, the operation commenced, and ended in a very bungling manner. Possibly the way I winced each time the sharp point pained me rendered my sister additionally nervous, or she may have been unaccustomed to delicate manipulation—under which head, I fancy, the extraction of a jigger's nest should be classed. Whatever the reason, she made matters worse rather than better by breaking the nest and scattering the contents; she then set to work to extract the separate germs by probing, when my screams collected a crowd around us. Among the curious was a Captain Armstrong, en route to Sacramento, where he was to have command of a river steamer. "What's the row?" he inquired. As soon as he heard, a quid of soft, moist tobacco was thrust into my ear. "There, now," he said, "don't you go and meddle with it; just let it be till morning. Tobacco juice is rank poison to jiggers or any other tarnation insect." After applying his remedy he sauntered off in quest of another quid, as he had removed the one he was then chewing to employ it as described.

The remedy he had so forcibly recommended and tangibly demonstrated was instantaneous relief to the acute agony which had been tormenting me ever since the previous night, and, as he had predicted, the inflammation and pain had entirely ceased by the next day.

Our steamer was called *The Gold Hunter*, but she did not give one the impression of a prosperous career.

We heard that she had belonged to the Government service, and when her boilers were worn out had been sold at auction as a worthless craft. Her falling into the hands of the Nicaragua Company was very characteristic. She was a prize eagerly seized by their agents. What did it matter if the machinery was in a bad state? A good bargain was of far more consideration, so they purchased her for a mere song, and patched her up at an equally low cost—the lowest possible—to convey between San Francisco and San Juan del Sud as much human freight as could be crammed on board. Twenty-five or thirty passengers might have managed to find elbow room in the saloon, but as we were four times that number the overcrowding was intolerable. Under these circumstances we felt ourselves to be extremely fortunate in having secured two deck-rooms corresponding with two on the other side of the funnel which were occupied by the captain and purser.

The children and nurse had rooms opening out of the saloon, a short narrow one, filled up by a table and stationary benches; several state-rooms lined the sides. There was no second cabin, as was usual in passenger vessels, consequently that class would be obliged to take their meals after we had finished, which was a far from pleasant prospect. The heat below was excessive, and the atmosphere always redolent of food. This horrible infliction we might partially escape by having deck-rooms. We sincerely pitied those who were forced to sleep in such stifling holes as the saloon cabins, and even of these there was a scarcity. Passengers took the precaution of bespeaking for themselves, if possible, portions of the table benches, and even floor, on which to sleep, so that they might, at any rate, know of some spot wherein to pass the night hours, either with or without mattresses, and from all appearances a vast majority would have to be content if not satisfied with the latter alternative.

Though there was absolutely nothing to retain one on shore, yet the hurry and helter skelter way in which we were driven on board, as if on the point of sailing, was one of those senseless acts too frequently practiced by those in authority over the passengers, as we failed to perceive the slightest indication of an approaching departure. Our chronicle, Jones, said the delay was caused by a deal of missing baggage, that ought by rights to have been on board hours before!

This piece of information did not surprise me; I only marvelled how any at all came safely to hand, for there was neither good management nor supervision of any description over the peons in charge, who came straggling along one after the other, carrying a trunk on their backs or bags under their arms. Every article was systematically relieved of straps or cords, which had been put on as a security against weak locks. Fifteen cents per pound weight was exacted on everything conveyed over the Isthmus, which payment was supposed to be a guarantee against loss. It was found that much of the baggage had been tampered with, and the only response to complaints was a fearful volley of curses and abuse. The poor steerage folk were the greatest sufferers, as their traps were mostly in bundles and sacks, which were easy of access.

When the gong sounded for dinner, we were still riding at anchor, with the prospect of being in the same position at supper-time. As the dining-table could only seat thirty, and there were over one hundred cabin passengers to be fed, we congratulated ourselves on being summoned to the first relay, as there would undoubtedly have to be several editions of each repast. One glance at the contents of the dishes dispelled all illusion. The provisions could not have been worse, everything smelt musty, and tasted the same, and even of this inferior quality there was a scarcity; and if this was so apparent at starting, how would it be before the termination of our journey to California?

If food was limited to rations, fresh water was no less so, and there being no condenser on board, the painful information reached us that nothing but salt water was to be procured for our toilet. I had submitted to much, but the risk of ruining my complexion was more than I could brook, and I forthwith made up my mind to make an appeal to the one who had the power to grant it. The captain's name was Bodfish; I immediately nicknamed him "Oddfish." He was a large, ferocious-looking man, yet I sought the lion in his den, and obtained the concession of a pitcherful of fresh water to be daily supplied to me. My need must have been urgent indeed and my courage great, to demand and obtain what I did!

As I surmised, we never got under way until supper-time. This meal was no improvement on the dinner, and we were glad to escape from the bad odour and sight of it to the luxury of our supposed cool, airy deckroom and the comfort of once more resuming a nightgown, the use of which we had almost forgotten.

Alas for the realization of our delightful anticipations! On entering the room we found it filled with vapour, without the possibility of remedy, as it proceeded from the boiler, which was situated directly beneath our cabin, a calamity we had not bargained for when selecting it, nor was a hint given of such being the case. We had been duped by the tricky purser, who was well aware that in that latitude it was uninhabitable. So after all our presumed luck was a snare and a delusion, and too late to be remedied, as every available nook had been reserved for those otherwise unprovided!

Jones, with a broad grin, brought out our bedding to the deck, where we passed the night in company with our gentlemen friends, who were to have occupied the cabin adjoining ours, which, being in a similar condition, had also to be vacated, and, like ourselves and a crowd of other people, they were obliged to sleep on deck, which was not amiss so long as the spread awning protected us from the dangerous influence of the night air and cloud of smoke and sparks emitted from the funnels. Unfortunately for us, the latter did some damage to the awning, which henceforth was furled before sunset, the risk to passengers being of minor importance to the destruction of the Company's property.

Our course was directed to Realejo, a little seaport in Mexico, which had been secured by the combined steam companies as a coaling station. We reached it on the evening of the third day; we heard the anchor drop while we were at supper. The hours for meals were breakfast from seven, dinner from one, and supper from six; unsatisfactory feeding appeared to proceed from early morning till late at night.

The approach to Realejo looked to us so uninteresting that we did not hurry our movements to obtain a nearer view. It was not the fare before us that induced us to linger at table a minute longer than was positively needful. The menu was far from elaborate, consisting of unpeeled potatoes (which constituted very nearly our only nourishment, as we knew them to be at least clean, if not of first quality), sardines in rancid oil, suspicious-looking rice, and still more suspicious-looking black treacle, the grave of many a cockroach I dare affirm, as I had on several occasions espied sundry wings and legs; the stewards alone could account for the absence of entire bodies!

We had heard boats coming to the side of our steamer, and distinguished the voices of strangers on deck, who were invited by the captain to have a drink of something stronger than tea or coffee. One of the new arrivals on entering the saloon rushed up to Mr. Higgin and grasped his hand with great enthusiasm. "Bless my heart! who ever dreamed of meeting you here?" he exclaimed, excitedly. Captain Ross was an old acquaintance, having for many years navigated the vessels belonging to Mr. Higgin's father, and the sight of a familiar face in such a remote spot was an agreeable surprise to both of them. The Captain at this time commanded *The Theodocia,* a three-masted ship, which had brought a cargo of coal from Newcastle. He was a gentlemanly pleasant person, and most kindly disposed towards his newlymade acquaintances, who soon became the recipients of many favours.

After some little conversation below, we all returned on deck, where an unexpected and agreeable surprise awaited us. Instead of the barren coast we had imagined, we were lying close to a number of small emerald islands, and were once more under the magic effect of tropical vegetation. The shore was fringed with groves of palms and other largeleafed trees, on which the moonlight gleamed and tinged with a silvery effect the graceful foliage. It was a lovely scene, this peaceful, motionless view. Not a breath of air stirred leaf, nor was a sound to be heard on shore; such a charming vista that we felt disinclined to leave it, but rather entertained the desire to sit there throughout the night, in order that we might contemplate its reposeful beauty. Others must have shared this impression, as I never knew so few disturbing elements among our crowd of passengers.

Unknowingly we had gone below, when we should have remained on deck to witness the entrance into the bay, which I, for one, very much regretted, for it must have been a pretty spectacle, and one well worth seeing.

BIBLIOGRAPHY

Caldecott, Maria Dundas Graham. *Journal of a Residence in Chile During the Year 1822, and a Voyage from Chile to Brazil in 1823.* London: Longman, 1824.

Calderón de la Barca, Fanny. *Life in Mexico.* Originally published in 1842. Reissued as *Life in Mexico: The Letters of Fanny Calderón de la Barca.* Ed. Howard T. Fisher and Marion Hall Fisher. Garden City: Doubleday and Company, 1966.

Beltrán de Santa Cruz y Montalvo, María de la Merced. *La Havane.* Paris: 1844.

Goritti, Juana Manuela. *El mundo de los recuerdos.* Buenos Aires: 1886. *Sueños y realidades.* Buenos Aires: 1865.

Hort, Dora (Mrs. Alfred). *Via Nicaragua.* London: Remington, 1887. Reprinted in 1987 by La Tienda el Quetzal, Conway, New Hampshire.

Pfeiffer, Ida. *A Woman's Journey Round the World.* London: Ward and Lock, 1856.

Prince, Nancy. *A Black Woman's Odyssey through Russia and Jamaica.* New York: M. Wiener Publishing, 1889.

Rousier, Ana du. *The Life of Ana du Rousier.* Ed. by Paz Riesco, RSCJ. Unpublished manuscript in the Nun's Library, Convent of the Sacred Heart, Santiago, Chile.

Sanborn, Helen J. *A Winter in Central America and Mexico.* Boston: Lee and Shepard Publishers, 1886.

Tristán, Flora. *Mémoirs et pérégrinations d'une paria,* Paris: 1838. This two-volume set was abridged and published in English as *Peregrinations of a Pariah,* 1833-1834. Translated, edited and introduced by Jean Hawkes. London: Virago, 1986.

Other Non-fiction from White Pine Press

A Woman's Gaze: Latin American Women Artists
Edited by Marjorie Agosín
264 pages $20.00

Backward to Forward
Essays by Maurice Kenny
176 pages $14.00

Ashes of Revolt
Essays by Marjorie Agosín
128 pages $13.00

Twilight of the Idols
Recollections of a Lost Yugoslavia
An Essay by Ales Debeljak
86 pages $10.00

Where the Angels Come Toward Us
Selected Essays, Reviews & Interviews by David St. John
246 pages $15.00

Among Buddhas in Japan
Essays by Morgan Gibson
158 pages $10.00

At the Edge
Nature Essays by Douglas Carlson
98 pages $9.00

Our Like Will Not Be There Again
Notes from the West of Ireland
Essays by Lawrence Millman
210 pages $12.00

Whereabouts: Notes on Being a Foreigner
Essays by Alistair Reid
206 pages $10.00

THE SECRET WEAVERS SERIES
Series Editor: Marjorie Agosín

Dedicated to bringing the rich and varied writing
by Latin American women to the English-speaking audience.

Volume 13
A SECRET WEAVERS ANTHOLOGY:
SELECTIONS FROM THE WHITE PINE PRESS SECRET WEAVERS SERIES
232 pages $14.00

Volume 12
XIMENA AT THE CROSSROADS
A novel by Laura Riesco
240 pages $14.00

Volume 11
A NECKLACE OF WORDS
Short Fiction by Mexican Women
152 PAGES $14.00

Volume 10
THE LOST CHRONICLES OF TERRA FIRMA
A Novel by Rosario Aguilar
192 pages $13.00

Volume 9
WHAT IS SECRET
Stories by Chilean Women
304 pages $17.00

Volume 8
HAPPY DAYS, UNCLE SERGIO
A Novel by Magali García Ramis
Translated by Carmen C. Esteves
160 pages $12.00

Volume 7
THESE ARE NOT SWEET GIRLS
Poetry by Latin American Women
368 pages $17.00

Volume 6
PLEASURE IN THE WORD
Erotic Fiction by Latin American Women
Edited by Margarite Fernández Olmos & Lizabeth Paravisini-Gebert
240 pages $19.95 cloth

Volume 5
A GABRIELA MISTRAL READER
Translated by Maria Giacchetti
232 pages $15.00

Volume 3
LANDSCAPES OF A NEW LAND
Short Fiction by Latin American Women
194 pages $12.00

Volume 1
ALFONSINA STORNI: SELECTED POEMS
Edited by Marion Freeman
72 pages $8.00 paper

OTHER LATIN AMERICAN TITLES

A WOMAN'S GAZE: LATIN AMERICAN WOMEN ARTISTS
Edited by Marjorie Agosín
264 PAGES $20.00

AN ABSENCE OF SHADOWS
Poems on Human Rights by Marjorie Agosín
212 pages $15.00

WINDOWS THAT OPEN INWARD:
POEMS BY PABLO NERUDA   PHOTOGRAPHS BY MILTON ROGOVIN
Translated by Bly, Maloney, Merwin, O'Daly, Reid, Vega, Wright
96 pages $20.00

NERUDA AT ISLA NEGRA
POEMS BY PABLO NERUDA   PHOTOGRAPHS BY MILTON ROGOVIN
Translated by Jacketti, Maloney & Zlotchew
127 pages $15.00

STARRY NIGHT
Poems by Marjorie Agosín
Translated by Mary G. Berg
96 pages $12.00

ASHES OF REVOLT
Essays by Marjorie Agosín
128 pages $13.00

MAREMOTO/SEAQUAKE
Poems by Pablo Neruda
Translated by Maria Jacketti & Dennis Maloney
64 pages $9.00   Bilingual

THE STONES OF CHILE
Poems by Pablo Neruda
Translated by Dennis Maloney
98 pages $10.00   Bilingual

SARGASSO
Poems by Marjorie Agosín
Translated by Cola Franzen
92 pages $12.00   Bilingual

LIGHT AND SHADOWS
Poems by Juan Ramon Jimenez
Translated by Robert Bly, Dennis Maloney, Clark Zlotchew
70 pages $9.00

VERTICAL POETRY
Poems by Roberto Juarroz
Translated by Mary Crow
118 pages $11.00   Bilingual

SELECTED POEMS OF MIGUAL HERNANDEZ
Translated by Robert Bly, Timothy Baland, Hardi St Martin and James Wright
138 pages $11.00   Bilingual

About White Pine Press

Established in 1973, White Pine Press is a non-profit publishing house dedicated to enriching our literary heritage; promoting cultural awareness, understanding, and respect; and, through literature, addressing social and human rights issues. This mission is accomplished by discovering, producing, and marketing to a diverse circle of readers exceptional works of poetry, fiction, non-fiction, and literature in translation from around the world. Through White Pine Press, authors' voices reach out across cultural, ethnic, and gender boundaries to educate and to entertain.

To insure that these voices are heard as widely as possible, White Pine Press arranges author reading tours and speaking engagements at various colleges, universities, organizations, and bookstores throughout the country. White Pine Press works with colleges and public schools to enrich curricula and promotes discussion in the media. Through these efforts, literature extends beyond the books to make a difference in a rapidly changing world.

As a non-profit organization, White Pine Press depends on support from individuals, foundations, and government agencies to bring you important work that would not be published by profit-driven publishing houses. Our grateful thanks to the many individuals who support this effort as Friends of White Pine Press and to the following organizations: Amter Foundation, Ford Foundation, Korean Culture and Arts Foundation, Lannan Foundation, Lila Wallace-Reader's Digest Fund, Margaret L. Wendt Foundation, Mellon Foundation, National Endowment for the Arts, New York State Council on the Arts, Trubar Foundation, Witter Bynner Foundation, the Slovenian Ministry of Culture, The U.S.-Mexico Fund for Culture, and Wellesley College.

Please support White Pine Press' efforts to present voices that promote cultural awareness and increase understanding and respect among diverse populations of the world. Tax-deductible donations can be made to:

White Pine Press

P.O. Box 236, Buffalo, New York 14201